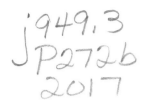

CULTURES OF THE WORLD
Belgium

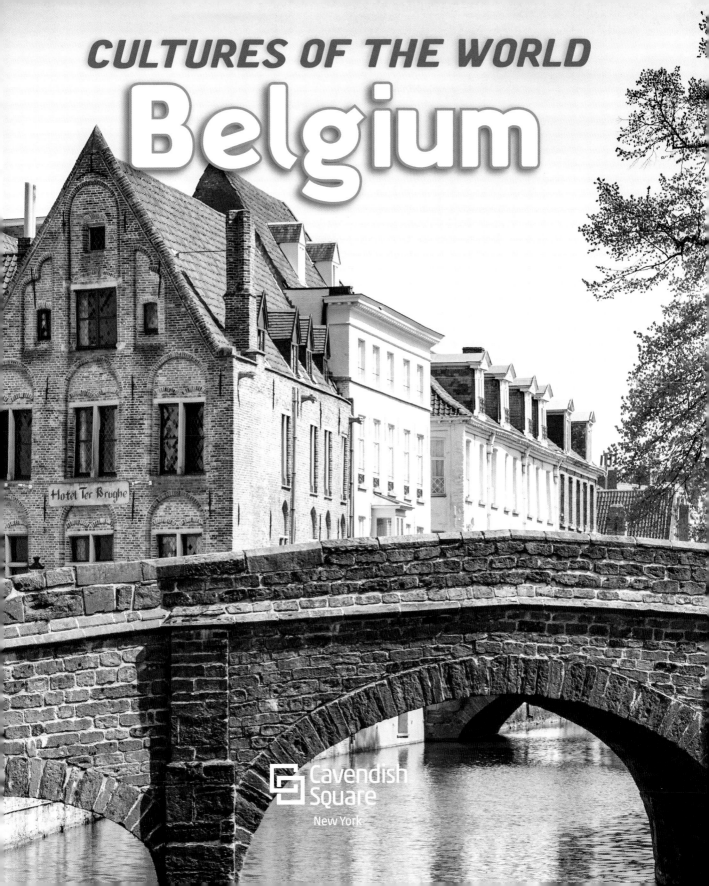

Hotel Ter Brughe

Cavendish
Square
New York

Published in 2017 by Cavendish Square Publishing, LLC
243 5th Avenue, Suite 136, New York, NY 10016
Copyright © 2017 by Cavendish Square Publishing, LLC

Third Edition

Cataloging-in-Publication Data

Names: Pateman, Robert.
Title: Belgium / Robert Pateman, Mark Elliott, and Debbie Nevins.
Description: New York: Cavendish Square, 2017. | Series: Cultures of the world | Includes index.
Identifiers: ISBN 9781502618351 (library bound) | ISBN 9781502618375 (ebook)
Subjects: LCSH: Belgium--Juvenile literature.
Classification: LCC DH418.P38 2017 | DDC 949.3--dc23

Writers: Robert Pateman, Mark Elliott; Debbie Nevins, third edition
Editorial Director, third edition: David McNamara
Editor, third edition: Debbie Nevins
Art Director, third edition: Jeffrey Talbot
Designer, third edition: Jessica Nevins
Production Manager, third edition Jennifer Ryder-Talbot
Cover Picture Researcher: J8 Media
Picture Researcher, third edition: Jessica Nevins

PICTURE CREDITS

The photographs in this book are used with the permission of: Alen Gurovic/Alamy Stock Photo, cover; Georgethefourth/Shutterstock.com, 1; Ian O'Hanlon/Shutterstock.com, 3; Pecold/Shutterstock.com, 5; Mikhail Markovskiy/Shutterstock.com, 6; Mark Renders/Getty Images, 7; Alexander Koerner/Getty Images, 9; symbiot/Shutterstock.com, 10; Peter Hermes Furian/Shutterstock.com, 12; leoks/Shutterstock.com, 14; Sergey Novikov/Shutterstock.com, 16; Shevs/Shutterstock.com, 17; Botond Horvath/Shutterstock.com, 19; Sergey Beketov/Shutterstock.com, 21; Anneka/Shutterstock.com, 22; Joostik/File:Lotharingia-959.svg/Wikimedia Commons, 25; Nicaise de Keyser/File:Nicaise de Keyser02.jpg/Wikimedia Commons, 26; Jan Willem Pieneman/File:De Slag bij Waterloo Rijksmuseum SK-A-1115.jpeg/Wikimedia Commons, 30; HUANG Zheng/Shutterstock.com, 31; Hulton Archive/Getty Images, 32; JOHN THYS/AFP/Getty Images, 34; Kartouchken/Shutterstock.com, 36; Julian Parker/Mark Cuthbert/UK Press via Getty Images, 38; NICOLAS MAETERLINCK/AFP/Getty Images, 39; JOHN THYS/AFP/Getty Images, 41; symbiot/Shutterstock.com, 42; topseller/Shutterstock.com, 44; Anneka/Shutterstock.com, 48; Philip Lange/Shutterstock.com, 50; TasfotoNL/Shutterstock.com, 53; pbombaert/Shutterstock.com, 54; Takashi Images/Shutterstock.com, 55; wim claes/Shutterstock.com, 56; Stephane Mignon/Moment editorial/Getty Images, 57; Kameel4u/Shutterstock.com, 58; Anton_Ivanov/Shutterstock.com, 60; Anibal Trejo/Shutterstock.com, 61; pavel dudek/Shutterstock.com, 62; EMMANUEL DUNAND/AFP/Getty Images, 64; LAURIE DIEFFEMBACQ/AFP/Getty Images, 65; FamVeld/Shutterstock.com, 66; Loop Images/UIG via Getty Images, 68; LAURIE DIEFFEMBACQ/AFP/Getty Images, 69; Thierry Dosogne/the Image Bank/Getty Images, 71; mastapiece/Shutterstock.com, 72; Sergey Rybin/Shutterstock.com, 76; Anneka/Shutterstock.com, 79; DeAgostini/Getty Images, 81; Peter Braakmann/Shutterstock.com, 82; Lonely Planet/Lonely Planet Images, Getty Images, 84; JOHN THYS/AFP/Getty Images, 86; Ssolbergj/File:Communities of Belgium.svg/Wikimedia Commons, 88; Alexander Tihonov/Shutterstock.com, 89; ONOKY - Fabrice LEROUGE/Brand X Pictures/Getty Images, 90; skyfish/Shutterstock.com, 92; Oleg Golovnev/Shutterstock.com, 95; daryl_mitchell/he Treachery of Images (This is Not a Pipe)/flickr.com, 97; Paulo Amorim/Moment Open/Getty Images, 99; Chris Jackson/Getty Images, 100; Bernard CHARLON/Gamma-Rapho via Getty Images, 101; skyfish/Shutterstock.com, 102; Matyas Rehak/Shutterstock.com, 104; Lee319/Shutterstock.com, 106; Florelena/Shutterstock.com, 108; Dean Mouhtaropoulos/Getty Images, 109; russ witherington/Shutterstock.com, 110; skyfish/Shutterstock.com, 112; DIRK WAEM/AFP/Getty Images, 114; skyfish/Shutterstock.com, 116; skyfish/Shutterstock.com, 117; Borna_Mirahmadian/Shutterstock.com, 120; travelfoto/Shutterstock.com, 123; Fanfo/Shutterstock.com, 124; Bastiaanimage stock/Shutterstock.com, 125; Lynn Watson/Shutterstock.com, 126; Elena Pominova/Shutterstock.com, 128; margouillat photo/Shutterstock.com, 130; Sara Winter/Shutterstock.com, 131; aomvector/Shutterstock.com, 137.

PRECEDING PAGE

A charming stone bridge spans a canal in Bruges, Belgium.

Printed in the United States of America

CONTENTS

BELGIUM TODAY

THINK OF BELGIUM AND WHAT COMES TO MIND? BELGIUM doesn't often make international headlines like, for example, Great Britain, or conjure up spectacular imagery like Switzerland. It isn't considered a powerhouse of Europe like Germany. People who are unfamiliar with Belgium might think of this small Western European country as a sort of "France Junior" or "Netherlands 2.0." Brussels, its capital, is the seat of the European Union (EU) and NATO (the North Atlantic Treaty Organization), and is sometimes referred to as the "capital of Europe." Belgium is indeed an important European hub of business and diplomacy, but where is *La Belgitude*—its Belgium-ness?

Independent since 1830, the Kingdom of Belgium is one of Europe's smallest, wealthiest, and most densely populated countries. It lies at an important crossroads of canals, rivers, railways, and highways, and Antwerp is one of Europe's most important ports. For the most part, Belgians are well educated and mostly Catholic, in culture and background if not always in practice.

It can be surprising to discover that for such a small country—and a monarchy at that—Belgium is an intricate patchwork of smaller parts, and in many ways, the parts are more powerful than the whole. The most important division is linguistic. Belgium is divided into two very autonomous regions—Flanders in the north and Wallonia in the south. The language of each region is different—French is spoken in Wallonia, while Flemish (a variant of Dutch) is used in Flanders. However, Belgium recognizes not two but three national languages: Flemish, French, and German, to accommodate the less than 1 percent of Belgians who live near the German border and speak that language. Administratively, in addition to Flanders and Wallonia, there is a third region, the multilingual Brussels-Capital Region. Flanders and Wallonia are each made up of five smaller provinces; the Brussels-Capital Region, however, has no provinces, and is not one itself.

Belgium, therefore, has one federal government, three linguistic communities, as they are called—the Flemish, the French, and the German-speaking regions; three administrative regions—Flanders, with its five provinces; Wallonia, with its five provinces; and the Brussels-Capital Region. Brussels itself is governed like a small city-state, with nineteen districts—each with its own mayor!

The façade of City Hall on the Great Market Square in Antwerp, Belgium, is aflutter with colorful international flags.

As if that isn't confusing enough for a country that is slightly smaller than the US state of Maryland, the territory of the mostly French-speaking Brussels-Capital Region is located wholly in Flanders, but is included in both the Flemish and French Communities; and the territory of the German-speaking Community lies completely within Wallonia.

It's important to recognize the fragmented nature of Belgium, because it is a major factor in the forces at work in Belgium today. For one thing, there are deep cultural and economic tensions between Flanders and Wallonia; so much so that the two regions operate as almost separate nations unto themselves, with the citizens of each identifying more strongly as Flemish or Walloon (wah-LOHN) than as Belgian. Indeed, political movements on both sides call for secession, though the push to make Flanders an independent country is by far the stronger of the two. A recent poll found that only a tiny minority of Walloons wanted Belgium to break up, but that if it were to

In Brussels, Walloon and Flemish Belgians march together against the possible separation of Belgium. The sign says, "One Walloon and one Fleming (Flemish person) equals two Belgians. Long Live Belgium!"

happen, about half of Walloons would prefer to see Wallonia become a part of France rather than go it alone as an independent country. All of which begs the question: why does Belgium even exist? The antagonism between the two main language regions dates to the nation's founding in 1830, when French was the language of the political elite and was Belgium's only official language. It was only in 1967 that a Dutch language version of the constitution was approved. Ironically, the economic situation has turned the tables and Flanders now holds the position of strength.

Since 1993, in an effort to address the concerns of Belgium's various constituents, the language communities and the administrative regions now have their own largely autonomous governments, and it's questionable, therefore, if this house divided against itself can continue to stand. Indeed, there have been ominous signs that the center cannot hold. In recent years, disputes between Flemish and Walloon politicians have, at times, paralyzed the Belgian government. In fact, Belgium earned the dubious distinction of holding the world record for the amount of time a democracy spent without an elected government. In 2010—2011, Belgium went without a government for 589 days when, following national elections, the opposing Flemish and Walloons were unable to agree on policy issues and form a governing coalition as required by the constitution. Many people expect Belgium to break apart, perhaps sooner than later.

In the midst of this conundrum, there are darker notes swirling in the gyre. In the twenty-first century, Belgium has made international headlines that no country would want. In the wake of several terrorist attacks in France in 2015, authorities traced the instigators to Belgium. The Brussels borough of Molenbeek, in particular—home to a large immigrant Muslim community— was found to have links to international extremist movements.

With media sources rushing to brand Brussels as "Jihad Central," critics charged the fragmentation of political authority in Belgium for allowing or even encouraging the undetected growth of both homegrown and imported extremism. In such a fractured political system, it's easy for government officials to pass the buck in circles, with the result being a fuzzy sort of inaction that would be comical if it wasn't so tragic. Brussels has six separate police authorities which have often not worked well together, if at all. Among the city's nineteen mayors from different parties, as well as from rich or poor districts, political distrust corrodes many attempts at communication and coordination.

The November 2015 attacks in Paris finally shocked the federal government of Belgium into sharpening its focus. It raised the terror alert to its highest level and, in an unprecedented move, imposed a security lockdown on Brussels—which essentially shut down the city for five days. One thousand police officers hunted for Salah Abdelsalm, the Belgian-born alleged mastermind of the attacks. Although the authorities arrested sixteen people, they failed to find Abdelsalm. This changed on March 19, 2016, when raids on apartments in Brussels resulted in Abdelsalm's arrest. Days later, on March 22, 2016, the Brussels airport departure lounge and a city metro station were attacked by suicide bombers, killing nearly forty people and injuring many others.

The aftermath of the attack on the metro in Brussels, March 2016

Will Belgium's new conviction be able to counter the passionate intensity of the "rough beast" in its midst? Will the fight against extremism unite the Belgian people or tear them further apart? As it was, anti-immigration fervor in Belgium was already on a political upswing even before the attacks on Paris and Brussels.

GEOGRAPHY

Autumn foliage and an old mansion reflect in a lake in Bruges.

1

BELGIUM IS OFTEN CALLED "THE Gateway to Europe." This phrase is often mentioned in relation to business opportunities, as well as to the country's three official languages and mix of cultures. It's also a reference to Brussels serving as the so-called "capital of Europe." Belgium is a founding member of the European Union, and the EU headquarters is in Brussels. When EU news bulletins are issued, European news media will often report that "Brussels announced" or "Brussels said" with the Belgian capital standing in as the symbol for most of Europe.

From a geographical perspective, Belgium occupies some prime real estate. The Belgian coastline faces the United Kingdom and the North Sea, one of the world's busiest waterways. Belgium is a frequent entry point to the continental mainland for travelers—there are five international airports—as well as for the commercial shipping industry. The port of Antwerp is one of the busiest in the world, and Belgium's important network of canals, rivers, and highways connects the country to Eastern and Western Europe.

Belgium, the Netherlands, and Luxembourg were once known as the Low Countries—in Dutch, *de Lage Landen*; in French, *les Pays-Bas*. They occupy coastal regions where much of the land is at or below sea level.

This map shows some of Belgium's most important cities, rivers, and regions, along with its bordering neighbors.

With an area of 11,781 square miles (30,513 square kilometers), Belgium is about the same size as Rhode Island and is slightly bigger than Maryland. Even at the widest point, it is only 180 miles (290 kilometers) across. On a map, the irregularly shaped country is sometimes said to resemble a bunch of grapes. The north and northwest parts of the country are low-lying; gently rising plateaus and hilly forests dominate the southern and eastern regions. Belgium shares borders with the Netherlands to the north, the Grand Duchy of Luxembourg to the southeast, Germany to the east, and France to the south and southwest.

FERTILE PLAINS AND UNDULATING PLATEAUS

Belgium can be divided into six main regions:

FLANDERS PLAIN On the coast of Flanders is a narrow belt of lowlands, reaching from the borders of France to the Schelde River. The area has many fine sandy beaches and dunes. Behind the dunes lie the polders (POHL-duhrs), land reclaimed from the sea and protected from floods by the natural barrier of dunes and artificial sea walls. The polders are formed by thin, sandy soil overlying clay and require heavy fertilization before they can be farmed.

Inland, the plains of Flanders extend southwest and are crossed by the Leie, Schelde, and Dender Rivers. Intensive farming and industrial development characterize this area.

THE CENTRAL LOW PLATEAU The plateau rises to a height of 700 feet (213 meters) in the south. It includes Belgium's best farmland, the result of the region's rich alluvial soils.

The Senne, Demer, and Dijle Rivers cross the plateau toward the Rupel River, ending in the Schelde River. Once covered with forests, the landscape has long been transformed by dense human habitation. Light industry is common along the region's impressive road network. While farmlands dotted with villages are a familiar sight, these increasingly merge into one another along major roads. Brussels, the capital of Belgium, lies at the center of this region.

THE KEMPENLAND PLATEAU In the north, by the Dutch border and between the Schelde and Meuse Rivers, rich farmland gives way to a region of sand dunes, scrub moorland, and coniferous forest. Just as in the south, coal deposits are mined in the region.

The Kempenland (Campine) is now a light-industrial district. The region also has an atomic research and nuclear power center, a recycling plant, and a large army base. Cutting through pleasant wooded countryside, the Albert Canal, which links the Meuse and Schelde Rivers, carries barge traffic on the way to Antwerp. Modern roads connect the region to Belgium's major cities and to Germany's industrialized Ruhr Valley.

The picturesque
city of Dinant
straddles the River
Meuse in Wallonia.

THE SAMBRE-MEUSE VALLEY This narrow but well-defined region is approximately 100 miles (161 km) long, but it is only about 3 to 10 miles (5 to 16 km) wide. Extending from the south to the north of Belgium along the Sambre and Meuse Rivers, the valley connects the central low plateau to the higher plateau of the Ardennes region. Coal mining used to be the main industry here, and it had supported other heavy industries; thus this region became one of the most populated in Belgium.

THE ARDENNES This plateau lies east of the Sambre-Meuse Valley. This was once a large mountain range, but the mountaintops were long ago worn down by glaciers. Today the Ardennes region consists largely of sandstone ridges, limestone valleys, and woodland hills rising above 1,000 feet (305 m). Close to the German border are some high hills: the Botrange is the highest point at 2,277 feet (694 m), and the Baraque Michel rises to 2,111 feet (643 m). The Ardennes region has excellent hiking trails, fast-flowing rivers, and winter snow, making it a major recreational area.

BELGIAN LORRAINE This region, located at the southeastern point of the country, rises to more than 1,300 feet (396 m). Part of the Paris Basin, soils here are far more fertile than in the bordering Ardennes. Farming and agriculture are the main occupations. Some iron deposits support steel mills and other industries, but this has not stopped the migration of its population to the cities.

Within these larger regions, there are several distinctive subareas that have their own geographical names. Hilly Hageland, east of Leuven, is famous for fruit and produces a variety of wines. The Borinage is the industrialized former coal mining zone around Mons. The Eastern Cantons (Ost Kantonen) region around the town of Eupen is Belgium's official German-language area with its own German-speaking parliament. Westhoek, in far western Flanders, is the location of the flat fields made infamous by World War I.

CLIMATE

Belgium has a reasonably gentle maritime climate due to prevailing winds from the west, which are warmed by the vast expanse of the Atlantic Ocean. Generally, summers are comfortably warm, at around 70 degrees Fahrenheit (21 degrees Celsius), without becoming overly hot. Winters are cold but seldom severe, with temperatures usually varying between 37°F (3°C) and 52°F (11°C).

Although the weather is typically mild, there are long periods of dull, gray days with abundant rain. Fog is common. Rainfall is rarely very heavy, but light rain can fall constantly for lengthy periods. When occasional winds blow from the east, across the Eurasian landmass, they bring more severe weather: snow, storms, and periods of unusual cold in winter or heat waves in summer.

The hilly terrain of the Ardennes in the east tends to be generally cooler and receives much more rain and snow than other areas. Only the summer months, from May to early October, are free of frost. Usually the area has heavy winter snows.

Belgium's river and canal system has played an important role in shaping the country's economy.

The Meuse (Maas in Flemish) is a gently flowing river that starts in eastern France and runs north into Belgium. It cuts a steep, narrow valley through the Ardennes, and it flows past the canyon town of Dinant before the Sambre River joins it at the fortress city of Namur.

A view of the Charles de Gaulle bridge over the Meuse in Dinant.

The Meuse continues to flow north, collecting other rivers as it goes. It runs into the Netherlands, and from there enters the sea south of Rotterdam. The Meuse is 575 miles (925 km) long, and ships can sail much of its length. Where the river is too shallow to allow ships to pass, canals have been cut. Of all the navigable rivers in Europe, only the Rhine is more important.

The Schelde (sometimes spelled Scheldt, or Escault in French) River is 217 miles (350 km) long and is a vital link in the European transportation network. The river starts in northern France and flows past Ghent (Gent), where it is joined by the Leie River. It then takes a northeasterly direction, eventually reaching Antwerp, which is Europe's second-largest port, despite being some 55 miles (88 km) inland. The building of new locks has enabled the harbor facilities to extend another 8 miles (13 km) downriver. Over fifteen thousand ships dock in Antwerp every year: that is more than forty every day. Although this number is around 10 percent fewer than thirty years ago, ships are now much bigger and almost three times heavier than before. In 2012, Antwerp handled 181.3 million tons (164.5 million tonnes) of cargo.

The warming influence of the sea makes coastal areas somewhat drier and sunnier than inland regions. Ostend, on the Belgian coast, averages about 1,760 hours of sunshine each year, while Brussels, less than 100 miles (161 km) away, gets around 1,585 hours.

In recent years global warming has resulted in hotter summers, colder winters, and a more tropical variety of rainfall, which increases the risks of flooding.

FLORA AND FAUNA

Belgium was once covered with deciduous forests. Oak was the most common tree, but beech, birch, and elm also thrived. Over the centuries, much of the original forest has been cleared for farmland or housing. The country's wildlife has been greatly affected by the destruction of the forests, but the forested Ardennes region is still a major refuge for animals such as boars, red deer, wildcats, and tree martens. The coastal region has its own rich fauna. This area is a vital resting ground for migrating birds and a winter home for many northern birds.

Belgium has one national park, the Hoge Kempen National Park, which opened in 2006. Made up of mostly heathland (a type of shrubland) and pine

Lightly rolling heathland is typical of the Kemperland region.

forest, it is located near the border with the Netherlands in the Kemperland (Campine) region. It is part of the Natura 2000, a network of nature protection areas in the European Union.

In addition, Belgium has numerous nature parks and protected wilderness areas. The Hautes Fagnes Nature Park, by far the largest, covers 167,655 acres (67,850 hectares) of boggy fenland east of the Ardennes. The much smaller Lesse and Lomme Park is Belgium's oldest reserve, protecting a beautiful stretch of Ardennes riverside. The Natural Park of the Valleys of the Burdinale and of the Mehaigne in the province of Liège includes twenty-three villages in more than 27,180 acres (11,000 ha) of protected land. On the coast toward the Dutch border, the Zwin Nature Reserve covers a tidal wetland area that is important for over a hundred different species of birds as well as the unique dune vegetation. Farther south, the Westhoek Nature Reserve has been set up to protect about 840 acres (340 ha) of sand dunes. As building continues along the coast, this might soon be the last area to retain the coast's original appearance. Despite these efforts, much of Belgium's wildlife, including some bat species and many wild plants, are still endangered.

CITIES

BRUSSELS (Brussel in Flemish, Bruxelles in French) is the capital of Belgium. The region includes nineteen communes (boroughs) of which one is the central, historical City of Brussels (also incorporating Laeken and the "European Quarter"). The whole Brussels metropolitan area spreads into several Flemish towns, including Vilvoorde and Zaventenm, where the international airport is located.

Brussels is at the hub of Belgium's roadway and rail networks. It is the headquarters of many international organizations, including NATO and the European Union. Its major industries include mechanical engineering, food processing, textiles, chemicals, electronics, and printing. Construction work is also very important, and there are several major international corporate headquarters in the suburban fields and forests just beyond the official city limits.

ANTWERP (Antwerpen in Flemish, Anvers in French) is Belgium's second largest city. It is the fifth busiest port in the world and, after Rotterdam in the Netherlands, the second busiest in Europe. In addition to being an important industrial city, Antwerp is also a major diamond center: 40 percent of the world's cutting and 70 percent of the polishing are conducted there.

LIÈGE (Luik in Flemish) stands where the Meuse and Ourthe rivers meet. It is Belgium's third largest city and was the site of the country's first coal mine. It was developed early as a commercial, financial, and industrial center. Various wars and battles over the years have destroyed much of the old city.

GHENT (Gent in Flemish, Gand in French) was a Roman city that grew into a great trading center during the Middle Ages. Magnificent buildings of that time still stand, including the town hall, cathedral, belfry, and cloth hall. Much of Ghent's charm and character comes from the many branches of the

A park in Brussels is adorned with geometrically-shaped bushes and trees, in the French style.

Schelde and Leie rivers that flow through the town. Ghent is also a thriving modern city, with a steelworks and factories that produce paper, chemicals, cars, and electrical goods. Although it is over 20 miles (32 km) from the sea, Ghent is linked to the coast by a canal and has its own harbor.

BRUGES (Brugge in Flemish) is sometimes called the Venice of the North because of its beautiful canals, bridges, monuments, and buildings—some of them dating from the fifteenth and sixteenth centuries. The city was once one of the greatest commercial cities in Europe. Today it is a major tourist town, but there are also breweries and other industries. Bruges is linked by a canal with the port of Zeebrugge about 7 miles (11 km) to the west.

MONS (Bergen in Flemish) was a wealthy trading city that suffered considerable bombing in World War II but remains colorful and appealing. It is especially boisterous during its Saint Wadru festival. Mons is the headquarters of SHAPE (Supreme Headquarters Allied Powers Europe), the military command center for NATO in Europe.

LEUVEN (Louvain in French) was an important center of the medieval cloth industry and has one of the world's most ornate city hall buildings. It is the home of one of Europe's oldest universities, founded in 1425.

NAMUR (Namen in Flemish) was historically one of Europe's most heavily defended citadels. The quiet city is now the capital of Wallonia, Belgium's French-speaking region.

CHARLEROI is located in the center of a coal basin and, accordingly, is nicknamed the Pays Noir (Black Country). Historically, the city has been the heartland of coal, metallurgy, glass, and other heavy industry. Today, however, it is economically depressed due to the decline of its traditional mining and steel industries. As part of its strategy for the future, the city is trying to transform itself from a "black country" to a green one.

MECHELEN (Malines in French) was once a powerful religious and cultural city famous for lace making. Today its focus is on furniture making and light industry. After its ongoing face-lift, it is likely to grow in importance as a tourist center.

OSTEND (Oostende in Flemish, Ostende in French) is Belgium's biggest coastal town and its main fishing and ferry port. The town commands a long stretch of sandy beaches that is popular with local vacationers.

Apartment buildings in the Flemish city of Ostend face the sea.

INTERNET LINKS

www.brussels.be/artdet.cfm
The official site of the City of Brussels has information on many topics, including pictures of Manneken-Pis in many of his outfits.

www.brusselslife.be/en/article/the-legends-of-the-peeing-kid
The legends of Manneken-Pis can be found here.

www.flanders.be/en
The official website of Flanders includes a "Discover Flanders" section.

www.lonelyplanet.com/belgium/places
This travel site looks at Belgium's various regions.

www.opt.be
The official Wallonia-Brussels site has pages and videos (some in English) on the cities, history, and culture of Wallonia.

www.rlkm.be/en/hoge-kempen
This is the site of the Hoge Kempen National Park, in English.

HISTORY

Ruins of the Orval Abbey in the Gaume region of Belgium date to medieval times.

2

BELGIUM IS BOTH A VERY OLD country and a relatively new nation. Archaeological finds reveal that various tribes lived in what is now Belgium for thousands of years. The modern nation of Belgium, however, only came into being in 1830. The country's history is deeply entangled with that of its neighbors, the Netherlands, France, Germany, and Luxembourg. Belgium has been part of huge empires or cut up into smaller states. It has also been the site of major events in European history, including many fierce battles. Because of its strategic location, it bears the unfortunate epithet "the battlefield of Europe."

ROMAN RULE

By 2000 BCE several distinct tribes had settled in Belgium. Among them were the Celts, an Iron Age people who probably came from central Europe. They intermarried with Germanic tribes from northern Netherlands.

The name Belgium signifies the country's ancient roots. It is taken from the Belgae tribes that populated the area more than two thousand years ago. The name relates to root words from several languages that mean "swollen with anger or battle fury." Ironically, this name was prophetic, as Belgium was the site of many battles over the course of history.

In 52 BCE, Julius Caesar and his Roman army conquered the area between the Seine and Rhine Rivers. They had fought a fierce battle against a tribe of people known as the Belgae, whom Caesar described as being the bravest of all the Gauls. The Belgae would give their name to Belgium many centuries later.

Under the Romans, Belgium became a rich trading center, and in time, most people adopted Roman customs. The towns of Tournai and Tongeren grew to be the most important Roman cities in the region. They each had a big army camp, and strong walls surrounded the cities to protect them against foreign invaders.

The Romans stayed for nearly five hundred years, but as Roman power declined, tribes of Franks from central Europe settled in the marshy lands to the north of the country. In 496 CE, Clovis I, king of the Franks, defeated the Romans. The Franks spoke a Germanic language, different from the Romanized speech of the south, so that even at this early date the inhabitants of future-Belgium were divided into two language groups.

Christianity was first taken to Belgium at this time by Irish and Scottish missionaries. They converted Clovis, but it was a second wave of Christianity in the seventh century that had more impact. It was at this time that many of Belgium's great monasteries were founded.

FROM TURMOIL TO TRADE

Between 768 and 814 CE much of Europe was united under the powerful King Charlemagne, and the Belgian area became a very important and prosperous part of the Holy Roman Empire, the medieval state that embraced most of Central Europe. Being a great organizer, Charlemagne built roads and developed the existing waterways. He promoted intellectual life and the arts.

When Charlemagne died in 814, his kingdom disintegrated and his sons divided their father's empire between France and Lotharingia, a swath of territory that included parts of today's Netherlands, Belgium, and western German and Switzerland. The region became more feudalized, and coastal areas suffered the raids of fierce Viking warriors from the north. Nobles lived in fortified castles, and towns built strong walls for protection.

Local counts and dukes grew more and more powerful and independent and became a major force in European politics. When the crusaders strode off to war against the Muslim rulers of Jerusalem, many present-day Belgian nobles gathered their armies and marched with them. Godfrey of Bouillon was one of the leaders at the siege of Jerusalem and was awarded the title "Steward and Protector of the Holy Sepulchre."

Beginning in the twelfth century, Flanders began to grow rich from its cloth trade. Flemish cloth was flexible, colorful, and soft. It was popular with rich and noble families throughout Europe. Flanders was soon using more wool than it could produce, and merchants traveled to Britain to buy more. Towns such as Ypres (Ieper), Ghent (Gent), and Bruges (Brugge) became great trading centers. They sold cloth and metal from south Belgium and bought wool, grain, smoked

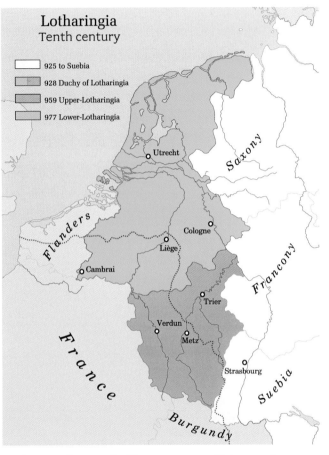

This map shows the medieval duchy of Lotharingia.

fish, furs, and timber from all over Europe. Soon the trading activities were regulated by strong guilds. As the merchants became wealthier, they were able to bargain for political rights through charters for their towns and increased their independence.

THE BURGUNDIAN PERIOD

Despite relative prosperity, times were still uncertain. Periods of bad weather brought famines, there was almost continuous warfare, and terrible plagues struck the population, killing thousands of people. During these periods of unrest and calamity, the dukes of Burgundy, who were influential noblemen, rose to power in the region. By the early fifteenth century they ruled over the seventeen provinces that now make up most of Belgium and the Netherlands.

The Battle of the Golden Spurs, which took place more than six hundred years ago, occupies an important place in Flemish history. In 1214 King Philip II of France defeated the Flemish and their English allies at the Battle of Bouvines, taking partial control of Flanders. Over the next hundred years the French became more powerful in Flanders and, by the 1300s, seemed ready to annex the land and make it part of France.

However, on the night of May 18, 1302, the citizens of Bruges rebelled, overpowering the guard and murdering everybody they suspected of being French. Encouraged by this news, ordinary people from all over Flanders gathered at Kortrijk (Courtrai) on July 11. The French knights were better armed, but the better-motivated Flemish people eventually defeated them and saved Flanders from French occupation, although only for a short time. The battle became known as the Battle of the Golden Spurs because afterward the Flemish gathered more than seven hundred golden spurs from dead French noblemen. May 18 is still commemorated as the National Day of Flanders.

Duke Philip the Good is the most famous of the Burgundian rulers. He reigned from 1419 to 1467, extending his domain in battle and improving the economy by reforming tax laws, banning English cloth, and promoting the Antwerp trade fairs.

As the free citizens grew more powerful through trade, they helped pay for the great town halls that are still admired in so many cities today. Rich merchants, the nobility, and the church started to invest their money in art, and a golden age of Flemish painters developed.

The fourteenth and fifteenth centuries saw some cities decline and others prosper. Brussels grew into the regional capital for the province of Brabant. The dukes of Burgundy occasionally held court there. This furthered the growth of the city. Bruges, which had been enjoying a "golden age" since 1100, began to decline when the Zwin, an estuary that formed the city's access to the sea, silted up around 1500. This allowed Antwerp to emerge as a new and dynamic trading center.

SPANISH RULE

When Philip's son, Charles the Bold, was killed in battle in 1477, his daughter Mary wed Maximilian of Austria, which brought Burgundian lands under the control of the Germanic Hapsburg family. The Hapsburgs were related to nearly all the royal families in Europe, and under Maximilian's grandson, King Charles V of Spain, present-day Belgium and the northeastern Netherlands became part of the powerful Spanish empire. It was one of the greatest empires Europe had seen since Roman times.

Cultural differences, however, were growing considerably. In the north, prosperity and education meant that many people had learned to read. The development of printing enabled local Christians to read the Bible for themselves instead of learning about Christianity from priests who were often corrupt. The result was Protestantism—a new form of Christianity that rapidly became popular in northern Germany and the Netherlands, including Belgium. When Charles V's Roman Catholic son, Philip, came to power, he saw Protestantism as a major evil. This led to thirty years of war. Initially, the Netherlands, including much of present-day Belgium, broke away from Spanish rule and set up its own independent nation. Spain eventually recaptured the area that is now Belgium (then known as the Spanish Netherlands). The people suffered considerable religious persecution. As part of peace negotiations with Holland, Antwerp, one of Europe's greatest port cities, was closed to trade. This created great economic problems for Belgium, which was left as a forgotten corner of the Spanish empire.

In 1659, King Louis XIV assumed power in France. He was determined to make the Spanish Netherlands part of his kingdom. The Spanish Netherlands became a battleground between the French and the newly independent Dutch, often aided by other European powers. In 1695, the French surrounded and bombarded Brussels, destroying much of the ancient city. However, a series of campaigns led by Britain's duke of Marlborough and Prince Eugène of Savoy finally forced the French out of the region.

In the Treaty of Utrecht (1713), France abandoned any claim to the Spanish Netherlands. The European powers, however, were uncertain as to what to do with the area. They did not think it could survive as an independent nation. As a result, Spanish Netherlands was given to Charles VI, the emperor of Austria, and the area became known as the Austrian Netherlands.

THE FIGHT FOR INDEPENDENCE

The 1789 Brabant Revolution briefly declared independence for the Belgian provinces of the Austrian Netherlands and established the United States of Belgium, which was later suppressed in 1790 by the Austrians.

In 1794, the Austrian Netherlands was suddenly conquered by France's new revolutionary government. French rule, under Emperor Napoleon Bonaparte, brought many important modernizing reforms. Industry was encouraged and the port of Antwerp, closed for many years, was reopened. The metric system and a new legal code were introduced, and Belgium was divided into nine departments.

However, the French were never popular, and their defeat in 1814 was generally welcomed. A few months later Napoleon once again marched into Belgium, only to meet his defeat at the Battle of Waterloo in June 1815. Some fifty thousand men died in that battle, which was one of the bloodiest and most decisive in European history.

At the Congress of Vienna in June 1815, the European powers reorganized Europe. They particularly wanted to prevent France from further expansion and from ever gaining control of the port of Antwerp. Under the influence of Great Britain, the Congress united the area with the Netherlands under the reign of William of Orange. However, in August 1830 a revolution broke out against Dutch rule, and by the end of the year, Belgium had declared independence.

Belgium's new constitution was considered dangerously progressive for the era. To counterbalance this liberalism, the founding fathers decided to look for a constitutional monarch. Several candidates declined. Eventually, German Prince Leopold of Saxe-Coburg-Gotha, an uncle of Britain's Queen Victoria, received the final approval of the major European powers. King Leopold I ascended the throne on July 21, 1831, the date now recognized as Belgium's National Day.

MODERNIZING AND COLONIZING

Few observers in 1831 really expected this artificial country to last more than a decade. However, King Leopold proved to be an able statesman and the economy prospered. Europe was being transformed by the Industrial Revolution and Belgium was in the ideal position to benefit from such industrialization. The newly independent nation had excellent harbors, both on the coast and inland, and seemingly endless coal fields. In 1835 the first railway line on the mainland of Europe was opened between Mechelen and Brussels. Equally important, Belgium's neutrality seemed to be accepted.

Leopold II ascended the throne in 1865. He believed that to finance Belgium's further development as a modern European nation and to raise the prestige of the country and the royal court, it should become a colonial power. He commissioned British explorer Henry Stanley to make a second trip to central Africa, carrying treaties of loyalty to the Belgian king. While there, Stanley persuaded many local chieftains to sign the treaties, effectively seceding sovereignty over their land to Leopold and allowing him to establish the Congo Free State (now the Democratic Republic of Congo), which he proceeded to rule quite ruthlessly as his personal property.

The territory yielded rubber, ivory, and other valuable resources, making the king wealthy enough to develop Belgian industry and to construct many great buildings, turning Brussels into a fashionable European capital. This was achieved at the cost of virtual slavery for the Congolese people, however, who suffered and often died under appalling conditions of forced labor. There were international protests against the treatment of the population. In 1908 the Belgian government was forced to take over the colony.

THE BATTLE OF WATERLOO

After a series of defeats in 1813 and 1814, France's emperor and master general, Napoleon Bonaparte, was exiled to the island of Elba off the coast of Italy. In 1815 he escaped and, incredibly, swiftly regained power in France, causing King Louis XVIII to flee. A coalition of foreign armies (including Britain, Russia, Prussia, Sweden, Switzerland, Austria, the Netherlands, and a number of German states) was assembled against him, and Napoleon knew that he had to strike first to knock them out before more could arrive.

On June 16, 1815, he hit first at the Prussian army at Ligny (in present-day Belgium). Thinking the Prussians were defeated, he then marched against his old foe, the British Duke of Wellington. Wellington cunningly positioned his troops behind an easily defended ridge just south of Waterloo village. From there he had the advantage of being able to look out over the enemy's positions.

Heavy rain delayed and confused Napoleon's attack plan. Hours later the French struck at Wellington's right flank. This was not supposed to be the main attack, but more and more soldiers were drawn into the battle. In the early afternoon Napoleon finally launched his main assault on the center of the allied line.

As the afternoon wore on, despite a desperate attack by Napoleon's elite Old Guard, the allied line held firm. Then, much to Napoleon's surprise, he found the Prussian army arriving to attack the French flank. They had not retreated after their earlier defeat, but

were now coming to Wellington's assistance. As more and more Prussian forces appeared, French hopes faded. Their weary army started to break up and flee south, and Napoleon himself was very nearly captured. The defeat at Waterloo ended Napoleon's rule as Emperor of the French (his official title). He abdicated four days later, and on July 7, coalition forces entered Paris and restored Louis XVIII to the throne. In October, Napoleon was exiled to St. Helena, a small tropical island in the South Atlantic, where he died in 1821.

The Battle of Waterloo left some fifty thousand men dead or injured, and changed the course of European history. It ushered in an era of relative peace, prosperity, and technological progress that lasted until the twentieth century.

In 1820, the Dutch King William I ordered the construction of a huge artificial hill on the battlefield, to be topped with an enormous lion statue, as a monument to the victory. The pyramid-like hill was built using the soil of Wellington's ridge, thereby greatly altering the lay of the land—to the everlasting regret of many tourists and historians. Today the Butte du Lion *(Lion's Mound)*/Leeuw van Waterloo *(Lion of Waterloo) remains a tourist attraction in Belgium.*

THE WORLD WARS

For much of the nineteenth century Belgium lived under the shadow of its powerful neighbor, France. By the beginning of the twentieth century it was Germany, newly emerged as a united nation, that gave greater concern. In August 1914 German troops marched across Belgian soil to attack France, plunging Belgium into World War I. The tiny Belgian army put up a brave fight

Albert I (1875-1934), King of the Belgians.

and even flooded some areas of their countryside to slow down the Germans while British and French troops were rushed in to help. By October 1914 the German advance was halted. Only a tiny corner of northwest Belgium remained unoccupied, but the Belgian king, Albert I, refused to leave it. (Today, Albert is still considered a hero. He is commonly depicted in statues wearing a simple soldier's helmet.)

Both sides dug a line of trenches that stretched from the Belgian coast through France and on to the Swiss border. Neither side could break through this defense system, and the war dragged on from one year to the next. It was a time of great hardship for the Belgians, most of whom were trapped in German-occupied territory.

The Great War of 1914 to 1918 (World War I), some of which was fought on Belgian soil, cost millions of lives on both sides without achieving victory for either. The Belgian cities of Ieper and Diksmuide and villages close to the front line were totally destroyed. It was 1918 before the arrival of large numbers of US troops finally helped to bring about the Allied victory.

After the war the right to vote was extended to all Belgian men; women's suffrage was granted only in 1948. The new government introduced major social reforms that included reducing the working day to eight hours, reforming taxes, and introducing old-age insurance. Although these changes helped to improve the standard of living for the majority of people, the worldwide Great Depression (1929—1939) caused considerable hardship and poverty. The 1930s also brought new political tensions, with the rise of Adolf Hitler and the Nazi Party in Germany.

In May 1940, Belgians woke to find that once again their country had been invaded by the German army. Using tanks and aircraft, the Germans were able to overrun the whole of Belgium in only eighteen days. This time the occupying army was to stay for five years, and in many ways the occupation was even more brutal and devastating than in World War I. Many Belgians were sent to Germany to work as forced laborers, and the Jewish population suffered unimaginable persecution.

In Belgium the population had to deal with several problems: a freeze in wages, high inflation, a rationed food supply, and a flourishing black market. The Germans fought resistance operations and bombings with violent counterterrorist activities and reprisals. World War II was a time of great confusion. In contrast to King Albert in World War I, King Leopold III quickly surrendered to the Germans. Although the king stayed in occupied Belgium, the Belgian government fled and set up a government-in-exile in London in October 1940. Belgian troops based there continued to fight alongside the Allies.

The Allies invaded northern France on June 6, 1944, D-Day, and by September they had liberated most of Belgium. However, Hitler launched a last desperate counterattack at Christmas 1944 in the Ardennes region. The American 101st Airborne Division was surrounded in the small town of Bastogne. When the Germans demanded its surrender, the US Army Brigadier General Anthony McAuliffe famously responded curtly with a single word: "NUTS!" The Americans fought bravely, losing almost eighty thousand troops in combat. After many more battles, the Germans in Belgium were finally defeated by the end of January 1945. Bastogne, grateful to the American troops, renamed its central square Place Général McAuliffe.

RECOVERY AND RECENT HISTORY

The postwar economy flourished, and Belgium became a founding member of the European Economic Community (now the European Union). Social conditions improved, but simmering differences between the major linguistic groups culminated in serious riots in 1968. To defuse tensions, the Flemish-, French-, and German-speaking communities were given responsibilities over their own educational and cultural affairs.

After a period of stagnation in the 1970s, the economy rebounded in the 1980s. However, economic growth proved much stronger in Flanders than in Wallonia where heavy industries languished. This disparity fueled continuing

Belgium has not been immune to the threat of terrorism that has spread across Europe in the twenty-first century. In fact, the country's role as a transit hub and transnational center has in some ways helped to attract Islamist militants. They, in turn, are recruiting new members from Belgium, with some success. In 2015, officials said about 350 to 450 Belgians had gone to fight in Syria and Iraq, the highest number per capita in Europe. For some reason, Sharia4Belgium, a radical Islamist group, had more recruiting success—particularly in Flanders—than similar organizations in other European countries.

Belgium is on high alert following the November 2015 attacks.

Many of the young people who joined the militants have been Belgian-born children of Moroccan parents, who may have felt marginalized in the European culture. A Belgian court in 2015 declared Sharia4Belgium a terrorist organization and jailed its leader. The group, which has since been dissolved, wanted to convert Belgium (and other European nations) into an Islamist state. To that end, the group sent many recruits to Middle Eastern war zones to fight with the Islamic State (ISIS), the extremist militant movement that arose in 2014. ISIS quickly seized control in parts of Iraq and Syria with the intention of creating a caliphate—a religious, political, and military Muslim authority, based on Sharia law, over all Muslims worldwide.

In January 2015, two terror suspects were killed and thirteen were arrested during an anti-terror police raid in the Belgian town of Verviers. The suspects had recently returned from Syria, where they fought for the Islamic State, and they were allegedly preparing an attack on police. Months later, in August, an apparent terrorist attack was foiled on a train in Belgium, when two US servicemen and a British civilian, who were traveling as tourists, overpowered a gunman. The assailant was a French Moroccan with terrorist ties. On March 22, 2016, Brussels was targeted in two deadly attacks, one at a city metro station, the other at the airport, killing many and wounding nearly one hundred people.

north-south linguistic conflicts that led eventually to federalism. A revised 1993 constitution divided Belgium into three highly autonomous regions: Flanders, Wallonia, and Brussels-Capital Region. In 2015 Belgium celebrated its 185th anniversary.

Also in June 2015, Belgium celebrated the bicentennial anniversary of the Battle of Waterloo with grand reenactments and other commemorative events. Britain and France also participated in observance of the two hundredth anniversary.

INTERNET LINKS

www.bbc.co.uk/timelines/zwtf34j
"The Battle of Waterloo: The day that decided Europe's fate" presented by BBC's iWonder series, is an easy-to-understand and well illustrated explanation of the battle.

www.cf2r.org/fr/tribune-libre/islamist-terrorism-in-europe-the-case-of-belgium.php
This French intelligence organization provides a thorough history of terrorism in Belgium.

www.cnn.com/2015/01/22/europe/belgium-terror-recruiting
This article examines why Belgium is fertile ground for terrorism.

www.lonelyplanet.com/belgium/history
This travel site offers a good overview of Belgian history.

news.bbc.co.uk/2/hi/europe/country_profiles/1002141.stm
BBC News provides a timeline of Belgian history.

www.theatlantic.com/photo/2015/06/reenacting-the-battle-of-waterloo/396479
"Reenacting the Battle of Waterloo" is a gallery of twenty-six photos of the bicentennial events.

GOVERNMENT

The Palace of the Nation in Brussels houses the federal parliament.

3

THE KINGDOM OF BELGIUM MAY be a small country, but it has a very complicated government and numerous political parties. Officially, the nation is a federal parliamentary democracy under a constitutional monarchy, which means it is made up of separate autonomous parts that are headed, but not ruled, by a king (or queen). Since 1993, the real power has been divided between three national and regional authorities: the national government, the three regions, and the three linguistic communities. Each administrative level has exclusive powers within its mandate and does not interfere with the other authorities, although their territories geographically overlap. There are also two levels of local government: provinces and communes.

Incredibly, Brussels is home to no fewer than five different parliaments: those of Belgium, the European Union, the Brussels-Capital Region, Flanders (combined with that of the Flemish Community), and the Francophone Community.

THE MONARCH

Belgium's head of state is the king or queen. Since the formation of the independent nation in 1830, there have been seven monarchs (as of 2015). King Philippe began his reign in July 2013 when his father King Albert II stepped down for health reasons after twenty years on the throne. The Belgian monarch's role is largely ceremonial, and carries great importance but little real power. The sovereign is the symbol of the unity and permanence of the nation. He or she influences political life not through personal authority but through guidance and suggestion. The monarch's interest, first and foremost, is the continuation, well-being, and international stature of Belgium, in accordance with the constitution. The monarchy is hereditary and heir apparent is Princess Elizabeth, Philippe's daughter.

NATIONAL GOVERNMENT

Queen Mathilde and King Phillippe of Belgium attend a gala marking the seventy-fifth birthday of Queen Margrethe of Denmark on April 15, 2015, in Copenhagen, Denmark.

Although the king is the official head of state, Belgium is ruled by a national parliament, which has responsibility for foreign policy, the national economy, justice, and defense. The Parliament consists of two houses. New bills, which make the nation's laws, have to be passed by both houses. However, the elected 150-member Chamber of Representatives is generally the major force. The 71-seat Senate is generally more concerned with longer-term legislation and constitutional matters. Representatives to both houses serve four-year terms.

The Senate's composition is rather complex: forty-one members must be Flemish speaking, twenty-nine Francophone, and one appointed German-speaking senator. Of these, one Flemish speaker and six French speakers must live in Brussels-Capital Region. Only forty members are elected by the public, according to a territorially defined system of electoral colleges.

Another thirty-one members are assigned by community councils. Curiously, the monarch's children are entitled to be extra senators once they are over eighteen years of age.

Elections for both houses are held at the same time and must be conducted at least every four years. As Belgian governments are complex coalitions of multiple parties, it is not unusual for the term to actually be shorter. All Belgians over the age of eighteen have the right to vote and are required to do so by law.

Prime Minister Charles Michel speaks during a session of the senate at the federal parliament in Brussels in January 2015.

POLITICAL PARTIES

There are currently some fifteen main political parties in Belgium, and other minor parties. Votes are by proportional representation with a minimum quota, so not all parties make it into Parliament, while others form multiparty umbrella groups to ensure a degree of mutual success. Parties relatively frequently change names and composition, and form alliances with other parties. However, in reality, most parties fall into one of three main groupings—Catholics/Christian Democrats, Socialist/Social Democrats, and Liberal/Liberal Democrats. Within each category there are yet different parties for French and Flemish speakers.

The Liberals include the party of Prime Minister Charles Michel (2014—), the French-speaking Reformist Movement (RM). It was created in 2002 from a coalition of parties, and tends to be fiscally conservative and socially liberal. The closest Flemish equivalent would be the Open Flemish Liberals and Democrats (VLD) Party.

The Christian Democrats—Christian Democrat and Flemish (CD&V) and the French-speaking Humanist Democratic Center (cdH)—are typically center-right, or conservative, on cultural, social, and moral issues, and support a market economy.

Socialist parties (the Socialist Party, or PS, and the Socialistische Partij Anders, or sp.a) are labor-based parties that typically concentrate on social welfare and social justice issues.

A party that has gained greatly in popularity since 2004 is the Vlaams Belang ("Flemish Interest," or VB). It is a right-wing populist and Flemish nationalist party, created in 2004 when its predecessor, the Vlams Blok ("Flemish Block") was declared to be a racist party. The VB focuses mainly on issues of Flemish independence—it seeks a peaceful secession of Flanders from Belgium—opposition to multiculturalism, and the defense of traditional Western values.

The leftist ecological, or green, parties—Ecolo in Wallonia and Groen in Flanders—support environmentalism, peace, diversity, and social justice within the framework of participatory democracy. They generally win a small number of seats in Parliament each electoral cycle.

REGIONS AND COMMUNITIES

The three regions—Flanders, Wallonia, and Brussels-Capital—reflect economic interests. Each elects a regional parliament and a minister-president. These regional parliaments take responsibility for planning infrastructure, water, energy, regional road development, and tourism

The Walloon
parliament meets
in May 2015.

within their areas. Each is highly autonomous. Although technically all foreign policy is decided at a national level, Flanders also sends its own representatives to many countries. The Wallonia Parliament meets in Namur, but Flanders has established its seat of government in Brussels.

The country is also divided into three linguistic communities, which reflect cultural interests. They are responsible for cultural matters, broadcasting, education, and health. These also have their own parliaments or councils, though the parliaments of the Flemish-speaking community (Vlaamse Gemeenschap) and of Flanders are de facto merged into one. The French-speaking Community (Communauté Francaise) covers most of Wallonia, including French-speaking institutions in bilingual Brussels, where it is based. The German-speaking Community (Deutschsprachige Gemeinschaft) encompasses roughly 76,000 people in Wallonia's eastern cantons around Eupen and has a council rather than a parliament.

There are nearly 13,000 councillors in Belgium, meaning that one in every six hundred people is directly involved in local politics. Most of these councillors are part-time politicians who carry out council business in their spare time.

Brussels is the home of the European Union (EU), a political-economic union of European countries, which has become a powerful force in Europe and the world. The EU was born in 1958 as the European Economic Community with just six member nations, which at first aimed simply to remove trade tariffs within Europe and create a common market. In 1993, it became the European Union and has now grown to twenty-eight members (as of 2015). The EU envisions the eventual establishment of common economic, foreign, security, and justice policies among the member nations. One major goal is to spread wealth and investment to help new member nations improve their prosperity and thereby gain stability.

Most of the important agreements and decisions are made by the Council of Ministers and the European Parliament. EU members are usually the foreign ministers of the member nations, but meetings might involve other ministers, depending on the agenda. Usually the heads of  *governments meet once or twice a year for a European Council. Decisions reached at these meetings are passed to the European Commission and the Parliament. The commission is the EU executive body, made up of professional bureaucrats selected by a long series of public examinations. It is nicknamed the Eurocracy and—given the twenty-four official languages—the teams of secretaries, translators, and accountants are very large. The Parliament is made up of 751 directly-elected members. Together, the two legislative branches of the EU attempt to develop common standards for member nations on a wide range of issues, from beach pollution to drinking water standards. In 2015, for example, the EU addressed challenges posed by the refugee crisis in Europe—huge numbers of asylum seekers pouring into Europe from Syria and other Middle Eastern countries.*

REGIONAL AND LOCAL POLITICS

Belgium is divided into ten provinces. Flanders and Wallonia have five provinces each. Although every province has its own directly elected provincial council and a governor appointed by the king, these have relatively minor political power compared with the regions or the much smaller municipalities and municipal boroughs. Most Belgians have a strong historical sense of local autonomy, and each of Belgium's 589 municipalities has a great deal of authority. Each commune has its own elected council and mayor, known as *burgemeester* in Flemish, *bourgemestre* in Belgian French. The bourgemestre is appointed by the king on the advice of the municipal council. It is not uncommon for high-profile mayors to also become ministers or national politicians at the same time. When this occurs, the actual day-to-day mayoral tasks are frequently delegated to city aldermen. Aldermen are elected by the borough council from among their own members.

The municipality is responsible for most matters of local interest, including the budget, utility rates, weddings, garbage collection, and the issuing of drivers' licenses. Until recently they even issued passports, but this has now been centralized to improve security.

INTERNET LINKS

www.belgium.be/en
This is the portal to the government of Belgium online, in English.

europa.eu/index_en.htm
The home site of the European Union has basic information, news, and even educational games.

www.monarchie.be/en
This home site of the Belgian monarchy has information about the monarch's role, the Belgian royal family, and more.

ECONOMY

Belgium is renowned the world over for its high-quality chocolates.

4

ECONOMICALLY, BELGIUM IS ALMOST two or even three separate countries. As a whole, it is one of the wealthiest countries in the world, but upon closer examination, regional differences tell a different story. The unemployment figures, productivity rates, and other economic indicators of Flanders, Wallonia, and the Brussels region vary a good deal. Flanders outperforms Wallonia and Brussels both in terms of employment and unemployment rates.

In general, however, Belgium enjoys low inflation, and its industries are increasingly modern and competitive despite intense global competition. The population is well educated and the workforce is one of the most productive in the world.

THE WORKFORCE

The population of Belgium is just over eleven million people. Statisticians classify those between the ages of fifteen and sixty-four as the potentially active workforce, around 5.2 million people. Some 8.5 percent of all active-aged Belgians are officially considered unemployed (in 2014), but the figures are lower in Flanders, at 4.5 percent; higher in Wallonia, at 10 percent; and highest of all in Brussels-Capital Region, 17.5 percent. On average, about 15 percent of the population live below the poverty line.

Today about 80 percent of the workforce is employed in service industries, such as education, transport, the hotel and hospitality business, banking, and finance. Belgium exports a growing number of services, with Belgian consultants and financial advisers working around the world. Belgians are productive workers who take pride in a job well done. The country's workforce is well trained and is often multilingual, which is the main reason so many foreign companies have invested in the country. Indeed, many secretarial and white-collar jobs expect candidates to speak a minimum of two or three languages fluently. In general, union membership is strong, union-employer consultative councils are often compulsory, and firing union representatives can prove very costly to an employer.

The Belgian government consults closely with workers, and wages and working conditions compare favorably with those in most other countries. The average workweek is thirty-eight hours, and Belgians typically have at least four weeks of vacation a year.

INDUSTRY

Being a small country, Belgium has a limited domestic market, and firms need to sell their goods overseas. Exports account for two-thirds of the country's gross national product (GNP), and in 2014, Belgium exported about $326 billion worth of commodities and services. About three-quarters of its trade is with other EU nations. This reliance on exports means that the Belgian economy can be seriously affected by international events. Belgium's main trading partners are France, Germany, the Netherlands, Great Britain, and the United States.

Industry now employs less than 20 percent of the labor force. Much of present-day industry involves importing raw materials and exporting finished or semifinished goods. The range of Belgian products is quite remarkable and includes cars, locomotives, textiles, plastics, glass, paints, industrial chemicals, explosives, fertilizers, photographic material, and medical drugs. Belgium is the world's leading manufacturer of industrial carpets, playing cards, and billiard balls, and is known worldwide for its fine crystal glassware, coffee appliances, chocolate, and breweries. In fact, the world's largest brewing company to date is Belgian.

High-technology industries have grown in importance. These include industries such as biotechnology, lasers, microelectronics, office equipment, robotics, medical technology, aerospace, and telecommunications.

Whereas the old industries had depended on the canals and railway lines to move their goods, these new industries are more concerned with being close to highways. Most also prefer to be in Flanders, close to port facilities. Today productivity in Flanders is roughly 20 percent higher, per person, than in Wallonia. The Flemish part of the country accounts for an even larger percentage of exports, producing some 70 percent of the total.

Although heavy industries, dependent on coal and iron, have traditionally been at the heart of the nation's wealth, these have declined over the last few decades and especially since the 1960s. This represents a prosperity shift from Wallonia, where the ebbing traditional heavy industries are centered, to the more modernized Flanders. The textile industry has also been severely reduced due to competition from developing countries where wages are far lower.

The old industrial plants, notably around Liège and Charleroi, are still struggling to modernize, though several former industrial giants have survived by becoming smaller and more streamlined. Nonetheless, Wallonia's economy remains relatively depressed, and in 2005 the Wallonia government launched what it dubbed the region's Marshall Plan. Since the original Marshall Plan funded the reconstruction of Europe after World War II, this name alone gives an idea of the scale of the challenge. The plan consists of massive public investments (around $1.6 billion) to promote and develop training, research, business support, innovation, and enterprise.

POWER AND TRANSPORTATION

Belgium's industry was traditionally powered by its coal fields. Coal production reached its peak in 1953 when 33 million tons (29 million metric tons) of coal were mined. By the 1980s it was down to 7 million tons (6.4 million t).

Cranes load cargo onto huge container ships in the port of Antwerp in Flanders.

Gas, nuclear power, and oil have since become far more important energy sources. One by one the coal mines were forced to close, causing considerable hardships in the coal-mining communities. The last Walloon coal mine closed in 1984. The Zolder and Beringen mines in Limburg continued operations for several more years but at last closed in 1992.

With no domestic oil or natural gas production, Belgium is therefore fully dependent on imports. However, due to its geographical location and transportation infrastructure, Belgium plays an important role in Europe's oil and gas supply chain. In fact, Antwerp has the largest petrochemical refinery in Europe. Nearly one-quarter of oil demand in Belgium is for fuel oil deliveries to international sea-going ships.

For years Belgium made a major commitment to nuclear power, and its first nuclear reactor went online in 1974, the first of seven. More than half of the country's electricity needs were provided by nuclear energy. However, in 2003, the government passed legislation committing to a phase-out of nuclear power generation. The law states that no new reactors will be built, and the existing plants are to be shut down by 2025. Two plants closed in 2015. This was accomplished amid a great deal of controversy, but the meltdown of Japan's Fukushima nuclear plant in 2011 gave a boost to antinuclear forces. The plan is to focus instead on renewable energy sources, notably solar and wind power. Whether renewables can replace nuclear in this decade is arguable, however, and many Belgians worry that a complete phase-out of nuclear power in so short a time will be impossible.

Because of the presence of good harbors and an excellent transportation network, Belgium has been described as the gateway to Europe. Antwerp ranks as the fifth busiest port in the world and the second busiest in Europe after Rotterdam; it is also regarded as one of the most efficient ports in the world. Considerable money has gone into expanding other harbors around the country. To transport goods to the port, Belgium has more than 2,000 miles (3,218 km) of railway lines, most of which are electrified. There is also a very extensive road system, including 1,072 miles (1,725 km) of toll-free expressways. Nearly 1,000 miles (1,609 km) of waterways are in regular commercial use, and Liège remains one of Europe's busiest river ports. The Meuse and the Schelde Rivers form the heart of this system, and they are linked by the 80 mile- (129 km) long Albert Canal. The country's largest canal, it was completed in 1939 to connect Liège with Antwerp and can handle barges weighing up to 2,000 tons (1,814 t). Transportation along the smaller Canal du Centre between La Louvière and Thieu is now four hours faster than before since the installation of a unique hydraulic boat lift at Strépy-Thieu that raises barges by a vertical 240 feet (73 m). Other important canals link Ghent, Brussels, and Bruges with the sea. Approximately 60 percent of goods are transported by road, 20 percent by rail, and the rest by boat.

Belgium is too small to require regular domestic air links, but it is well connected with flights to other countries. Brussels (Zaventem) is the most important of Belgium's five international airports, and Belgium is the European hub for several international freight-forwarding corporations. Belgium's national airline, SABENA, was declared bankrupt in 2001, but there remain three locally based airlines, SN Brussels, Virgin Express, and VLM. SN Brussels offers many useful connections to African cities.

INTERNET LINKS

www.cia.gov/library/publications/the-world-factbook/geos/be.html
The CIA World Factbook gives up-to-date statistics on Belgium's economy.

www.fao.org/ag/agp/agpc/doc/counprof/belgium/belgium.htm
The UN Food and Agriculture Organization offers facts and figures about agriculture in Belgium.

www.world-nuclear.org/info/Country-Profiles/Countries-A-F/ Belgium
The World Nuclear Association provides an overview of nuclear power in Belgium.

ENVIRONMENT

Rental bicycles wait for takers at a Villol station in Brussels.

5

A S A HIGHLY INDUSTRIALIZED AND densely populated country, Belgium has its share of related environmental challenges, such as air, water, and soil pollution. Like most Europeans, Belgians are generally interested in conservation and want to be good environmental stewards. Indeed, the country has made significant gains in air quality in recent decades. Energy usage is decreasing, and improved wastewater treatment, especially in urban areas, has made for cleaner surface water. Nevertheless, much remains to be done.

In the 2014 Environmental Performance Index (EPI), Belgium ranked 36th out of 178 countries, and was the lowest ranked of the Western European countries. The EPI evaluates a country's performance in nine key areas: air quality, water and sanitation, water resources, health impacts (child mortality), climate and energy, agriculture, forests, fisheries, and biodiversity and habitat. Of those, Belgium scored an excellent 100 percent for water and sanitation, and 99.65 for health impacts. However, its environmental performance was less impressive in the other areas, with fisheries scoring a 0. In that, Belgium

Belgium's renowned beer industry may be experiencing the effects of climate change. In 2015, one of the country's most celebrated brewers said it was scaling back production because recent weather extremes had shortened the production season and made brewing conditions more volatile. Its brewing season used to last from October to May but shrunk to the period between November and March or April.

was hardly alone, however; virtually no country met the target for fish stocks, pointing to the enormous problem of over-exploited and collapsed fisheries worldwide.

As a member of the EU, Belgium must strive to meet some of the world's highest environmental standards. Failure to do so results in consequences. For example, in June 2015, the European Commission summoned Belgium to the EU Court of Justice over its failure to meet air quality standards, specifically its persistently high levels of the dust particles known as PM10s. These mostly result from human activities such as transport, industry, and domestic heating, and can cause respiratory problems, lung cancer, and premature death. The report acknowledged Belgium's improved track record on air quality in recent years, but stated that three regions—Brussels, the Ghent port zone, and the Roeselare port zone—showed continued failure to meet the targets.

Belgium's environmental policy is also influenced by the Aarhaus Convention of 1998. This UN environmental agreement guides the interaction between the public and public authorities in processes concerning local, national, and transboundary environment issues. It provides for unfettered access to information, public participation in decision making, and access to justice in cases of a party's failure to adhere to the environmental law.

GREENHOUSE GASES AND CARBON EMISSIONS

The effects of climate change are already being seen in the region's unpredictable weather—colder winters and hotter summers. Climate change is a result of global warming, caused by the emission of greenhouse gases, notably carbon dioxide, which are produced when fossil fuels such as natural gas, gasoline, and other petroleum products are combusted. Like most developed nations, Belgium has ratified the Kyoto Protocol, which is designed to slow down greenhouse gas production. To work toward this goal, the government is confronting the problem on both large (macro) and personal levels.

On the personal level, public education programs are conducted to show, for example, how to save money as well as reduce energy consumption by regularly defrosting refrigerators, using high-performance lamps, or washing clothes on low-temperature cycles. Washing machines are taxed according to their energy-efficiency grading, prompting individuals to choose power-efficient appliances. Each of Belgium's three regions has a series of grants available for encouraging fuel-efficiency measures in the home, such as installing loft insulation (usually fiberglass matting in rolls), double glazing windows, and converting heating systems to high-efficiency condensation-type gas boilers. Despite relatively low sunshine figures, tax and grant incentives mean that home owners are starting to find it profitable to install solar roof panels.

Steam rises from the cooling towers of the Doel Nuclear Power Station near Antwerp. The plant was taken offline in August 2014 due to unexplained malfunctioning and possible sabotage but was restarted in November 2015.

On a macro level, considerable investments have been made in wind turbines, though some local people dislike the giant windmills as they feel these spoil their scenery. Belgium's electricity-generating system is now highly dependent on nuclear power. Although these produce no greenhouse gases and are thus considered useful in decelerating global warming, they are potentially very dangerous if an accident should occur. Furthermore, nuclear waste is extremely toxic and difficult to dispose of. In 2002, under pressure from environmentalist parties, the government agreed to scrap all nuclear power stations by 2025. This further pushes the need to develop renewable and sustainable energy sources.

GARBAGE, RECYCLING, AND REUSE

Garbage collection systems vary greatly within Belgium as each town or municipality organizes its own. Nonetheless, it is common for most towns to encourage a division of waste into various classes to allow for easy and efficient recycling. There might be special collection days for paper, plastics and metals, garden and other organic waste, and general refuse. Householders typically pay for waste collection by the number of bags, but the charge for the

Trash bins in a Brussels train station are color coded for recycling.

collection of recyclable waste is cheaper per bag than for general garbage. This encourages people to think green.

Glassware is rarely included in household garbage collections. Instead people are urged to use bottle-bank collection points for jars and wine bottles. Other bottles, especially beer bottles, have a paid deposit, so the consumer is financially rewarded to take those bottles back to the seller for washing and reuse.

Each region (Flanders, Wallonia, and Brussels) has its own recycling agency. These are also charged with educating the public to better understand the waste management systems.

ECO TAXES

Since 1993, eco taxes have been applied to encourage recycling and inspire an environment-friendly mentality among citizens and businesses.

Batteries are a common source of hazardous waste in family garbage. Belgium's high-profile campaign to recycle batteries has been aided by eco taxes and also by a major awareness campaign. As a result, almost every family keeps old batteries out of their trash, using the special envelopes provided by BEBAT, the battery recycling organization, instead.

Since 2001 a recycling contribution eco tax has been added to the price of most electronic equipment. The tax has been cleverly calculated so that the tax charged will rise with the degree of difficulty with which a product can be recycled. This encourages manufacturers to think about the environment when designing their devices and packaging. Businesses selling electronics now must also think about their products' disposability. That's because "take-back" legislation provides that any customer buying a qualifying product can take to the store the old version that he or she is replacing.

As in most European countries, the tax on gasoline is extremely high, which is why a gallon of gas costs around $6, or €1.35 per liter (in 2015). The idea of these high prices is to encourage people to use public transportation and thus reduce both traffic congestion and the emission level of greenhouse gases that cause global warming.

In Belgium, however, this approach is not especially successful because the public transportation system is not usually convenient enough. There is another series of taxes on cars, charged according to their fuel efficiency: if a car has low carbon dioxide emissions and high fuel efficiency, the owner will pay much lower rates.

This tram is part of the Brussels tramway network for public transportation.

WATER

Belgium is home to several major commercial mineral springs and the world's original spa at, yes, Spa. If one goes to a restaurant in Belgium and asks for a glass of water, one will always get bottled or mineral water. Waiters will be shocked if tap water is requested instead and might refuse to serve it. This is purely convention and clever economics. In fact, Belgian tap water is perfectly good to drink and is subjected to around fifty different tests and checks to ensure that it is safe for consumption.

Yet even at home many Belgians drink bottled water. In 2004, a tax was added to plastic bottles in an attempt to fund their recycling and discourage the use of disposable bottles. However, this caused annoyance among Belgium's powerful water bottlers. The tax was removed in mid-2005.

THE NORTH SEA

Belgium has 41 miles (66.5 km) of coastline facing the North Sea—a sensitive ecosystem under a great deal of pressure from intense human activities, and surrounded on three sides by densely populated, industrialized countries. Rivers flowing into the sea carry effluent and sometimes toxic industrial discharges. Some ecologists suggest that such pollution might have

North Sea
harbor seals

contributed to the viral diseases that decimated the North Sea seal populations in the 1980s and that struck again in 2002.

Considerable quantities of oil and gas are extracted from deep beneath the North Sea, while its waters are crisscrossed by some of the world's busiest shipping routes. Both these activities add to the threat of water pollution, whether from small oil spills or catastrophic accidents involving tankers or oil rigs.

Historically, fishing has been a major industry in the North Sea and around 5 percent of the world's total fish catch is still caught here. To preserve fish stocks, stringent EU quotas on catches have been imposed over recent decades. This has partly reversed the devastating effects of previous overfishing. However, many fish-species populations have not rebounded as quickly as had been predicted. Scientists suspect that this might be linked to a slow rise in sea temperatures due to global warming. Cold-water fish such as cod are increasingly found farther north in subarctic waters, and some predict that they will become extinct in the North Sea over time. Meanwhile, warmer water fish, such as the mullet, squid, and lobster, are becoming more common.

Belgium's short coastline culminates at Het Zwin, a stretch of protected salt marshes that attract thousands of waterbirds, including migrating swans and reed geese. Eagle owls can also be spotted here. Farther south are some beautiful dunes and many miles of wide, sandy beaches. Despite the unpredictable weather, beaches are backed by heavily developed tourist resorts aimed mainly at the domestic market of weekend visitors, accounting for about thirty million visits per year. This economically important recreation and hospitality industry is directly impacted by environmental concerns over the quality of the North Sea water. At times the sea is even considered unsafe for swimming. However, the Flemish Environment Agency now marks the beaches to alert swimmers to the water quality. Smiley, sad, or neutral face symbols are posted according to the results of seawater tests. Samplings are carried out at least twice weekly in summer. Meanwhile, a department of the Royal Belgian Institute of Natural Sciences (RBINS) studies the ecosystems of the North Sea, using mathematical modeling techniques to assess the condition of the marine environment.

The beach of the coastal village of De Haan in Flanders is considered one of the most beautiful beaches in Belgium.

INTERNET LINKS

www.climateadaptation.eu/belgium/agriculture-and-horticulture
This site predicts the effects of climate change in Belgium.

www.eea.europa.eu/soer-2015/countries/belgium
The European Environment Agency has an up-to-date report on the status of Belgium's environmental issues.

epi.yale.edu/epi/country-profile/belgium
The Environmental Performance Index is thoroughly explained on this site, including Belgium's country profile.

BELGIANS

6

WHO IS A BELGIAN? IN THIS country, that is a trickier question than one might suppose. The problem of defining nationality gets back to the bilingual divide at the heart of Belgium's identity. The population of some 11,325,000 consists of two major language communities: the Dutch speakers (Flemish), which make up about 60 percent of the population, and the French speakers (Francophone), which account for 40 percent. There is also a small community of German speakers, and although less than 1 percent of Belgians speak German, it is nevertheless one of Belgium's three official languages.

Ethnically, Belgians follow much the same pattern, with Flemish people making up 58 percent of the population; Walloon comprising 31 percent; and mixed or other ethnicities accounting for some 11 percent.

Belgium is a small country with a large population. In fact, it's one of the most densely populated countries in the world. Consider this: Belgium is physically about the size of the US state of Maryland. However, its population puts it more on par with Ohio, which is four times larger.

TWO DIFFERENT PEOPLES

The Flemish and the Walloons make up the vast majority of Belgians. The Flemish mostly live in the north and speak Flemish, a version of Dutch. Those Belgians who speak a version of French are termed Francophones. They live mostly in Brussels and Wallonia. The term "Walloon" is often used to describe people from Wallonia, but to most Belgians it refers more specifically to speakers of various thick and often hardly intelligible dialects of French. Walloons trace their ancestry back to the Celtic Belgae tribes who were reputed to be ferocious fighters. After the Belgae were conquered by Rome about 52 BCE, they started to integrate with their Roman invaders, so their language became Latinized.

Centuries of intermingling have resulted in there being no immediately apparent racial or physical difference between Flemish and Walloons, although people from Wallonia tend to be marginally shorter than those from Flanders. In the last century, immigration into Wallonia has further added to the Mediterranean looks of some Walloons, while typical natives of Flanders are somewhat more likely to be blond-haired and blue-eyed in the Viking-Germanic mold.

In reality, the deep divisions in Belgian society are almost entirely a matter of language and culture. For centuries French was the legal and court language, and historically Francophones did not think well of their Flemish-speaking neighbors. Flemish elites in cities like Antwerp and Ghent would often associate the French language with prestige. By the nineteenth century, Wallonia, the home of most mining and heavy industry, was vastly more economically powerful than Flanders.

Flags wave in front of City Hall in Mons, a provincial capital in Wallonia.

Flemish people who did not speak French were unable to understand legal procedures. In several infamous cases during World War I, soldiers were court-martialed and excecuted for failing to carry out orders that they simply did not understand because they did not speak French. Understandably, this caused a great sense of injustice and a newly vibrant Flemish literature scene pushed heavily for linguistic equality.

During the twentieth century this was not only achieved, but the whole economic balance of the country shifted. Flanders, once the poor half of Belgium, is now considerably wealthier than Wallonia. Increasingly, more Flemish people have started to feel that their enterprise is wasted by having to help support the economically ailing south. Others, however, realize that as a rich part of the EU, an independent Flanders could end up subsidizing poorer nations from Poland to Portugal, so they consider it better to subsidize Wallonia, which is closer to home and familiar.

THE GERMANS, BELGIUM'S THIRD GROUP

German was recognized as one of Belgium's official languages in 1963. However, there are only around seventy thousand German-speaking Belgians. They live in the Ostkantonen, a small strip of land around the town of Eupen, close to the German border. This region was given to Belgium by the Treaty of Versailles after World War I to help make amends for the war. The area was briefly annexed by Germany during World War II but was returned to Belgium after the Allied armies liberated the country in 1944.

Most people from this region describe themselves as Belgians who happen to speak German. Most are bilingual, in French as the children start learning French in the first grade and then another language as they grow older. People in this region still feel proud about their German culture and language.

The German minority have benefited from the ongoing struggle between Belgium's two larger language groups, and they have acquired considerable independence without ever really campaigning for it. There are a German radio station and television service for the area and a few small German newspapers. Economically, the area has strong links with Germany. The large German city of Aachen is just across the border, and many people commute there to work and shop.

The Belgian city of Eupen, where German is commonly spoken, is about 10 miles (15 km) from the German border.

HOW THE BELGIANS SEE THEMSELVES

Sometimes it is hard to see what keeps Belgium's linguistically divided peoples together. In fact, there are several common characteristics that cross the Francophone-Flemish barrier. Both communities are overwhelmingly, if only nominally, Roman Catholic, sharing a curious mixture of conservative mind-set with outwardly liberal attitudes. Both communities might dislike one another, but both prefer each other to their other near neighbors: Francophone Belgians find French people typically arrogant, while the Flemish tend to see their Dutch neighbors as humorless and tightfisted. On either side of the linguistic divide, Belgians delight in a quietly indulgent good life, with fine food and plenty of it washed down with some of the world's best beers.

Both communities show an entertainingly deadpan style of conversation where the borderline between grumbling and humor is often hard to spot.

By necessity, living in such a fragmented society has made Belgians particularly adept at compromising. Living in a small country, many Belgians have a remarkably open-minded view of the world. Most Belgians consider themselves to be reasonably easygoing but at the same time independent and capable of being quite stubborn when the need arises.

By Western Europe's high standards, Belgium has traditionally been seen as a place where mild corruption and nepotism, or favoritism, are the norm. There have been some improvements in recent years, and in 2014 Belgium stood at the 15th position, together with Japan, in the 2014 Transparency International's Corruption Perceptions Index. (For comparison, Denmark ranked number 1, or least corrupt; the United States ranked 17; and North Korea and Somalia tied for last place, or most corrupt, at 174.) Nonetheless, having the right connections remains very useful and is still very much part of the Belgian way of life. Giving corporate gifts and inducements is rarely seen to be corrupt, but merely oiling the wheels of personal interactions.

IMMIGRANTS AND FOREIGNERS

Belgium's healthy economy, its many multinational organizations, and its pan-European institutions attract many people from other countries. As of 2012, about 13 percent of the officially registered population was foreign-born, but other studies estimated the true rate of immigrants and their descendants in the Belgian population at 25 percent. Of these people, 49 percent were of European ancestry and 51 percent were from non-Western countries.

In the 1960s immigration was encouraged by the government, as Belgium had a shortage of labor. The first waves of immigrants came mainly from Italy and, later, Morocco and Turkey. Many became Belgian citizens and are a part of the nation's increasingly mixed community. Others integrated into Belgian society but chose to keep their original nationality. At first some did this to avoid doing national service in the Belgian armed forces, though such service is no longer required. People from the former African colonies add another dimension to the ethnic mixture.

Following the November 2015 terrorist attacks in Paris, investigations quickly turned to the Brussels neighborhood of Molenbeek. Several of the suspects, including the alleged mastermind, had been based in that part of Belgium. Law enforcement personnel were not surprised. Numerous highly publicized terrorist events of the twenty-first century were perpetrated by young men from Molenbeek.

Sint-Jans-Molenbeek (or Molenbeek-Saint-Jean, in French), one of nineteen municipalities in the Brussels-Capital Region, is home to some 93,000 residents. It has two distinct districts, refered to as the higher and lower regions, and the lower section is impoverished and overcrowded. It houses a large community of Muslim immigrants, mostly from Morocco and Turkey—in some pockets more than 80 percent of the residents are Muslims—and over the years it has become a haven for radicalized jihadists. After the Paris attacks, international news media took to labeling the neighborhood "Jihad Central."

Why Molenbeek? Immigrants have been moving to the gritty Brussels suburb for decades, and naturally, most of them are not terrorists, nor do they support terror. However, in recent years, a significant number of the region's young people traveled to Syria to fight on behalf of ISIS (also known as the Islamic State, ISIL, and Daesh), the militant extremist group attempting to create a harsh interpretation of an Islamic state in the Middle East and beyond. Those young men often returned to Molenbeek as hardened jihadists.

The Brussels authorities, meanwhile, turned a blind eye to a situation they were well aware of. Some critics blame the fragmented nature of Belgium's government—Brussels alone has nineteen mayors! The lack of a strong central authority, paired with a tolerant culture that refused to counter the negative influences of imported extremism, is seen as inadvertently creating a perfect refuge for terrorists.

Belgian laws protect the ethnic and religious freedoms of all people, but social and cultural problems remain. Some immigrants have found it difficult to integrate with the rest of the population, and there is a tendency to group together in certain areas. Immigrants tend to be most concentrated in Brussels, particularly in the Molenbeek district.

Many ordinary Belgian citizens see immigration as one of the most important issues that affect the future of their country. There is a common perception that foreigners are responsible for a variety of socioeconomic problems and petty crime. Such sentiments are most extreme in Flanders, even though that region has the lowest percentage of resident foreigners or immigrants. The extremist Vlaams Belang Party has taken advantage of this. Its predecessor party, Vlaams Blok, campaigned under the slogan "Our Own People First" until it was outlawed as racist. Vlaams Belang has become one of the biggest parties in Flanders.

People protest at a meeting of the Flemish far-right party Vlaams Belang with French right-wing politician Marine Le Pen.

INTERNET LINKS

www.belgiumtheplaceto.be/happy_famous_belgians_introduction.php
This site lists many famous or important Belgians in various categories, with links to short biographies.

www.euro-islam.info/country-profiles/belgium
This site offers an in-depth look at the recent history of Muslim immigration to Belgium.

www.politico.eu/article/molenbeek-broke-my-heart-radicalization-suburb-brussels-gentrification
This is a fascinating first-person account of living in Molenbeek.

LIFESTYLE

A family enjoys a picnic during a trip to the Walloon city Dinant.

THE BELGIAN LIFESTYLE IS MUCH
the same as that of any other
Western Europeans. Like people
pretty much anywhere, they place great
importance on family, friends, and
food. According to the Organization for
Economic Cooperation and Development
(OECD)'s Better Life Index for 2015,
Belgium performs well in many measures
of well-being relative to most other
countries. Belgium ranks above average
in work-life balance, income and wealth,
housing, civic engagement, education
and skills, life satisfaction, health status,
jobs and earnings, and social connections.
However, the country ranks below average
in personal security.

In January 2003,
Belgium became the
second country to
recognize marriage
between same-
sex couples. Child
adoption rights
for gay couples
were approved in
December 2005.

HOUSING

There is a popular expression that goes like this: "Every Belgian is born
with a brick in the stomach." This reflects the dream that many Belgians

have to design and build their own homes. Traditionally, old Flemish houses had attractive Dutch-style stepped side gables that created distinctively photogenic town centers. These days, however, despite Belgium's rich architectural heritage and the people's passion for designing their own homes, popular building styles are surprisingly dour and functional. Houses typically are made of brick with tiled roofing, often finished with a coat of whitewashed plaster. In suburban areas luxurious "villas" (single-family houses) are relatively common, along with cheaper duplex units and apartment buildings. In cities, apartments and connected townhouses are more common.

Particularly high taxes imposed on the purchase and sale of houses means that once Belgians have bought or built a home, they are unlikely to move again. Therefore, choosing where to buy or build is very important. Generally, the most popular areas to live in are in the outer suburbs or the villages just beyond city limits. This has resulted in many Belgians commuting long distances to work, causing extensive rush-hour traffic congestion. The trend of building in the increasingly crowded countryside has also caused more and more houses to appear along once-rural roads, undermining the very appeal of these areas. Differences between rural and urban lifestyles are also diminishing, although regional differences and identities remain pronounced.

JOBS, CARS, AND CLOTHES

As in most successful capitalist nations, there is considerable social pressure to find good jobs, establish strong careers, and gain promotions. However, most Belgians feel that one works to live rather than lives to work. So although Belgians work hard to get ahead, they will not necessarily be keen on advancement if it requires giving up their holidays or weekends.

Advertising encourages the pursuit of name-branded material possessions. However, showy displays of wealth and status are frowned upon. To impress others, one's choice of status symbols should be carefully targeted and not ostentatious. Foreign visitors often notice the remarkable number of expensive automobiles and jump to the conclusion that Belgians are extravagant with their cars. In reality, a very high percentage of these fine vehicles are company cars. Employees who drive them could rarely ever afford to buy such expensive models. Both businesses and employees find that a leased company car is a handy way for everyone to avoid paying taxes on new cars.

A car is towed from an accident scene in Denderleeuw in Flanders.

Many people acknowledge that Belgians are not particularly safe drivers. Despite strict laws to make roads safer, there are often bad accidents. Unless the police are in sight, many drivers tend to ignore the minor regulations. Cars weave through traffic at high speeds, even in places where that means rattling over old cobblestoned streets. Non-European drivers need to be aware of the terrifying "right-priority" rule. This gives priority at any unmarked junction to the vehicle that arrives from the right, even when there is a very small lane leading onto a major through road. The country also has to grapple with the hazards of drunk and reckless driving. It is not surprising, given these problems, along with some very poor road signs, ambiguous pedestrian priorities, and hard-to-understand expressway junctions, that in 2010, Belgium had the second worst per-capita road fatality rate in Western Europe (after Portugal).

If Belgians put less emphasis on clothing than the French or Italians, they still like to look good. Particularly in Brussels, it is evident that people invest a great deal of care and money in their appearance. The clothing budget of most Belgians is spent on good quality apparel. The dress code is quite formal. In offices, men are still expected to wear jackets, although in winter, as a concession to the cold, a jacket might be replaced by a nice wool sweater. It is quite acceptable for women to wear pants to work.

SOCIAL INTERACTIONS

Belgians are not shy, but they are typically quite reserved. It would be considered unusual for a stranger to try to strike up a conversation in public. In stores it is normal good manners to say "good day" to a shopkeeper or checkout clerk before proceeding with a purchase. However, it is uncommon to ask "How are you doing?" to those you do not already know. When introduced to strangers, Belgians are generally formal and polite, but they do not expect effusive interest. Generally, Belgian friendships must be won over a considerable period, and breaking into a social group takes some effort and commitment. Friendly neighbors nod greetings to one another or stop to chat outside their homes, but they wouldn't necessarily expect to be invited inside even after several years of acquaintance. Although people vary greatly, it is unusual to drop in on a Belgian friend without telephoning ahead. When visiting, it is typical to bring flowers, wine, or a small gift, depending on the occasion.

Between strangers, a handshake is usually appropriate. The two parties introducing themselves simply utter their names. Colleagues greeting each other at the start of another day at work might also shake hands in a relaxed

Belgium has a highly developed system of social services and spends more on social protection than the European average. Belgians receive a family allowance, free education and scholarships for advanced education, health care, pensions, and welfare benefits for the unemployed.

A low birth rate and an excellent health care system have brought a noticeable change in the average age of the population. At the start of the twentieth century, one out of every fifteen Belgians was over sixty. Today the figure is one out of every five. Belgian men can expect to live to an average age of seventy-eight, women to eighty-four. The most common causes of death are cancer and heart disease.

The aging of the population has created some serious social and economic problems. The country faces a rising bill for nursing and pensions. In addition, higher unemployment, a lower birth rate, and more single-parent families make the Belgian social protection system weigh heavily on the state budget. A restructuring to moderate costs was begun in 1981. A portion of the health-care costs are now chargeable to patients. Welfare payments to the longtime unemployed are being gradually lowered.

way. Close friends and family are more likely to kiss one another. The full Belgian kiss greeting is three times on alternating cheeks. The procedure is often shortened to a single cheek peck, especially when there are many people to greet. Indeed, in Flanders some people consider a single kiss to be more generally appropriate, though rules are not hard and fast. Men are less likely to kiss one another than women, but male relations and close friends may do so. When answering the telephone, most Belgians simply announce their name or say "Hallo?"

A teacher instructs his students on a field trip to the Grand Palace of Brussels.

EDUCATION

The Flemish-, French-, and German-speaking communities each have their own separate education ministry, and education is given in the regional language. Education is compulsory until the age of eighteen, and one out of every four students continues their education beyond this point. Schools in Belgium are run both by the government and by private organizations, notably the Catholic Church. Generally, Catholic schools have the best reputation for educational standards. Funds for both state and private schools are provided by the government, so education is essentially free, except in international schools, which are very expensive but mostly cater to expatriate families. Nonetheless, parents must still fund school trips and pay a small charge for photocopies, library fees, composition books, and a school-rules manual. Parents are also expected to buy all schoolbooks, and many children will get some money back by selling these at the end of the year. The curriculum for both primary and secondary education is guided by education inspectors.

Belgian children usually start kindergarten at the age of three, but many working parents enroll their toddlers in preschool even before that age. At age six children proceed to primary school, which lasts for six years. When they are twelve years old, they move into secondary school, which involves a great deal more of research-based study and a choice of difficult subject options. Normally, only those who complete the sixth grade of secondary school education are eligible for university, though vocational school students can qualify by completing an extra (seventh) year of school. Students who fail exams have to repeat the year's curriculum. Those who do not do well in academic schools are encouraged to seek work apprenticeships or entry to a vocational school, which develops practical skills.

Belgium has a five hundred-year history of university education, with the Catholic University of Leuven being a notable international center of learning and research. Today a network of nineteen universities and other institutions of higher learning educate some 100,000 students a year. Students have to complete two cycles—one of general studies and one of specialized studies—that last two to three years each before being awarded a degree that leads to a professional life. Generally, only around 40 percent succeed in passing the first year. During the last few decades increased close cooperation with Belgian industries has helped various universities join world leaders in scientific research and training.

ROLE OF WOMEN

The last few decades have seen a remarkable feminization of the workforce in Belgium. In 1970, only 32 percent of active-aged women worked. This has now risen to 57 percent. Laws passed in 1978 guarantee men and women equal legal and social opportunities, and equal wages for equal work; nevertheless, in reality, women still face a gender pay gap, earning less than men in the same position. Claims of sexual harassment, or women receiving unfair treatment at work, are taken seriously, although there is often a marked difference between what Belgians and Americans consider as sexist.

A high percentage of working women are employed in the services and the government sector, and others work in industry and agriculture. Although there has yet to be a female prime minister, women hold about 39 percent of the seats in the national parliament. Highly educated women hold key positions in judiciary and diplomatic fields, and the government campaigns to encourage women to aim for positions as decision makers and managers in industry, the media, and the business world.

Government policy encourages working women to combine professional and family life: child care helps women return to work quickly if they wish, but it is also possible for mothers to take up to four months leave to care for their new babies. Especially among older working couples, however, it is still relatively unusual for a man to stay home to look after young children.

THE FUTURE

Despite the high level of autonomy given to the federation, linguistic differences and tensions remain overwhelmingly Belgium's most sensitive issue. Many locals doubt whether the country will survive as a single unit for their lifetimes—or even for the next decade.

Unemployment and national debt remain major concerns for many Belgians. Those who have lost their jobs in the old industrial areas and lack any other qualifications are facing up to the fact that they might be out of work for years. Young people attending university are also worried about finding work. As people age, they are becoming increasingly nervous about their pensions: controversial plans to prevent early retirement at the age of fifty-eight and to change many pension benefits caused a one-day national strike in 2005, the first in twelve years.

Immigration is another issue that disturbs many people; there is a widely held view that too many foreigners are coming to live in Belgium. This is reflected in recent election results that gave considerable support to right-wing parties promising to control immigration.

Taxes are the fourth great concern. Nobody likes taxes, but in Belgium, tax dodging is seen as something of a national sport. Since many people try to avoid taxes, the government is moving to generally reduce taxation, hoping that in the end more people will pay so that the books will still balance. A less-than-successful "tax amnesty" in 2004 tried to persuade Belgians to bring home their secret savings from foreign bank accounts, notably in low-tax Luxembourg. Such funds are routinely called "black cash" in Belgium. The Belgian Parliament tried again in 2013, offering a tax amnesty for a few months, but the success of that attempt is unclear.

Crime is less of a worry than in the United States and in other parts of Europe. One reason is that the possession of weapons is strictly controlled. But there is a rising concern over crime. The many expensive cars and the relative ease of escaping across unsecured national borders into neighboring countries have encouraged an increased frequency of carjacking.

In 2015, Belgium had a murder rate of 1.1 per 100,000 population. (For comparison, the homicide rate in the United States in 2015 was 5.2 murders per 100,000 people.) However, the uptick in terrorist incidents caused great concern, not only in itself, but also because it was associated with a corresponding uptick in hate crimes against minorities. Social problems of graffiti and assault on public transportation employees are also increasing.

INTERNET LINKS

diplomatie.belgium.be/en/policy/policy_areas/human_rights/ specific_issues/gender_and_women_rights
This Belgian government page discusses gender and women's rights.

www.healthworkscollective.com/stevenshie/130271/health-reform-trust-what-makes-health-care-work-success-story-belgium
This short article compares the health-care systems in Belgium and the United States.

www.oecdbetterlifeindex.org/countries/belgium
The OECD Better Life Index page on Belgium presents findings in rating general well-being.

RELIGION

A statue of the Virgin Mary and the Baby Jesus adorns a wall in Bruges.

8

A T THE START OF THE FIFTH century, the warlike Franks moved into Belgium and overran most of the Roman settlements there. One of the Frankish leaders, King Clovis, converted to Christianity in the year 496. A diocese was established at Tongeren, and churches were built around the country as the new religion spread.

The seventh century saw Christianity spread more rapidly, especially during the reign of the Frankish king Charlemagne. Over the centuries Benedictine monasteries and abbeys became great cultural centers and major landowners, the clergy being allied with the local nobility. The eleventh century has been called the Age of Faith, when people in both Flanders and Wallonia, and indeed in most of Europe, held unquestioning belief in Christianity.

EMPTY CHURCHES

Belgium is predominantly a Roman Catholic nation and the last country in northern Europe to have a Catholic monarch. Most national holidays are based on Christian holy days, notably Christmas, the Assumption, and Easter. Most of Belgium's greatest festivals, particularly their fabulous carnivals, are related to religion, albeit distantly.

Despite the common use of the term Catholic as a social label, few people regularly attend church. Attendance is slightly higher in Flanders

In Belgium it is still relatively common to see small street shrines dedicated to the Virgin Mary in niches on homes and at rural roadsides. Many of these shrines are well maintained and sometimes decorated with flowers.

than in Wallonia, and higher in villages than in urban communities. The church plays a role at funerals, and a priest typically visits bereaved families of the dead. Cemeteries themselves are generally plots of civic land not linked to a religious establishment. Although many Belgian couples enjoy holding a wedding ceremony in an old church, the legal act of marriage must always be conducted in the local town hall.

Despite the small congregations, Belgian churches still demonstrate a remarkable vitality, helped by the fact that the Belgian government pays the priests' wages. Congregations are involved in a whole range of community activities, and the buildings are well tended as well as decorated inside with candles and flowers. Churches also sponsor considerable missionary work and aid projects around the world.

RELIGIOUS ORDERS

Monasteries, convents, and abbeys, where people can remove themselves from the material world and devote their lives to God, are a small but important part of Belgian religious life. Although some of the abbeys and monasteries have closed, there are still people who seek life in a religious order.

From the middle of the eleventh century onward, religious orders owned some of the richest farmland in Belgium. They became profitable commercial concerns. They used their wealth to help the poor and were important patrons of the arts. Many of the monks were themselves magnificent artists who have left wonderful treasures in the form of manuscripts, metalwork, statues, and paintings.

Many different monastic orders are represented in Belgium, but it is the Cistercians who have probably had the greatest impact. In 1098, Robert of Molesme felt that the Benedictines had become too lax. So he left with a few followers to found the Cistercian order (at Cîteaux in France). By the end of the twelfth century, the Cistercians had over five hundred monasteries. The order emphasized the importance of manual work and had a great impact on farming techniques throughout the country. Trappists, the strictest of all Cistercians, even made a rule to maintain silence except when absolutely necessary.

Many monasteries today are best known for their brewing of beers and making of cheese. Brewing was originally important for health reasons, as water supplies were often unsafe to drink. Later, beer was sold to fund the restoration and upkeep of the institutions, especially after the destruction caused by the French invasion after the French Revolution. Belgium's most famous beers are still produced by the Trappist abbeys of Orval, Rochefort, Chimay, Westemalle, Westvleteren, and Achel.

The *Begijnhofven* (buh-GEYEN-hoVEN, *Beguinages* in French) were special religious homes where women could enjoy fellow female company and security within a religious atmosphere without taking vows. Mostly confined to the Netherlands and Flanders, the movement is believed to have been started by Lambert le Begue to help women who had lost husbands and sons in the Crusades. The *Begijnhof* communities consisted of a church, infirmary, weaving center, and small, individual houses around a safely enclosed courtyard. The beautiful Begijnhofven of Flanders are now recognized collectively by UNESCO as world heritage sites. There are wonderful examples of the Begijnhofven in Bruges, Lier, Diest, Tongeren, Leuven, and Turnhout.

Medieval white houses are part of the *beguinage* in Bruges.

PILGRIMAGE

Belgium's most important Catholic pilgrimage is to Scherpenheuvel, in Flemish Brabant, on the first Sunday of November. The story goes that some time in the early sixteenth century a shepherd was wandering in the fields near Scherpenheuvel when he found a statue of the Virgin and Christ Child attached to an oak tree. When he tried to remove the statue, he became fixed to the ground. This was taken as a sign that the statue wished to remain there, and a chapel was built to house it. Although the statue was later destroyed, the place remained an important pilgrimage site, and kings often went to pray there before going into battle.

In 1933, in the tiny hamlet of Banneux near Liège, young Mariette Beco claimed to see eight visions of the Virgin Mary. The village has since become a place of pilgrimage. The visions are very controversial, though, as some people think that the claim of the encounter was made to boost the income of the Beco family, who still runs local gift shops.

Saint Hubert, a little town in the center of the Ardennes, is a pilgrimage site particularly popular with hunters. According to legend, Saint Hubert was hunting there when he saw a stag with a shining cross hanging between its antlers. A voice told him to take up missionary work, and he eventually became the Bishop of Liège. Today Saint Hubert is the patron saint of hunters.

Sick people might still make pilgrimages to the cathedral at Halle, a small city south of Brussels, which has a black Madonna statue that is believed to work miracles for people who pray before it.

LIVING MUSEUMS

Over the years, a great deal of energy has gone into building and decorating Belgium's churches and cathedrals. Today these religious sanctuaries are guardians of a considerable part of Belgium's national heritage. Although primarily religious buildings, they are also recognized as cultural centers that house different forms of expression. Many treasures from the very earliest days of Christian history have been lost, but a few wonderfully handwritten Bibles, some decorated in ivory and gold, have survived.

The 1400s were noted for the great works of Flemish artists, many of which were commissioned for churches. Probably the most wonderful example is *The Adoration of the Lamb*, painted by Jan and Hubert van Eyck for the Cathedral of Saint Baaf in Ghent. The Antwerp Cathedral has a later but equally impressive treasure in two magnificent paintings by Peter Paul Rubens. Great numbers of church treasures were destroyed during the Reformation by fanatical Protestants. These Protestants are remembered as iconoclasts because they burned icons, which they considered to be signs of the church's forgetting of Christ's true message. The Saint Leonarduskerk in Zoutleeuw is the only major church interior in Belgium to have retained its full medieval splendor to this day.

The Adoration of the Lamb (1432) is the center panel of the Ghent Altarpiece.

Compared with their interiors, church buildings have fared much better and now form an important part of the nation's architectural legacy. The earliest churches were built in the Romanesque style with small windows and thick walls that bore all the weight of the structure. These grew larger and larger, reaching an extraordinary climax in Tournai and Nivelles, whose twelfth-century cathedrals are captivating Romanesque masterpieces. From the thirteenth century the "new" French Gothic style was used in Belgium. By employing buttresses and vaulted roofs, churches attained breathtaking new height and splendor—vast windows flooded the interiors of the buildings with light. Over the next century work started on many of the great cathedrals that still stand in Belgium, including Antwerp's Onze Lieve Vrouw Cathedral and the Cathedral of Saint Michael and Saint Gudula in Brussels, which look remarkably similar to the much more famous Notre Dame Cathedral in Paris.

OTHER RELIGIONS AND SECULARISM

Islam is the second-largest religion in Belgium. There are estimated to be upwards of nine hundred thousand Muslims in Belgium, many of Turkish or

When German troops occupied Belgium in 1940, life became very difficult for everybody. Initially the Jews were not persecuted, but in June 1942 things started to change. Jews were forced to wear the Star of David on their clothing, publicly identifying them as being Jewish.

That summer the Germans asked for Jewish "volunteers" to go off to work in labor camps. As the daily conditions of life in Belgium were very severe, many people, believing the German propaganda, thought they might be better off in the camps. In reality, these places were concentration camps where the inmates were cruelly treated and then horribly exterminated. As frightening rumors spread back to Belgium, the number of volunteers dried up, and the Germans started to hunt down the remnants of the Jewish population for forcible deportation to the death camps.

Many Belgians showed great bravery in helping Jewish families hide, and an underground movement was set up to offer information, money, and a vital ration card. Special covert efforts went into hiding Jewish children. They often had to be isolated from their families and sent to boarding schools and convents, or to live with other families. This was a very traumatic experience, particularly as they had to change their names and did not know where their parents were. After the war, many Jews, mainly in Antwerp and Brussels, started searching for surviving deportees and investigating the whereabouts of missing family members.

Despite those heroic efforts on behalf of Belgian Jews, there was also considerable complicity on the part of Belgian officials at all levels in aiding the persecution, deportation, and murder of Jews. It was only in 2012 that the Belgian Prime Minister Elio Di Rupo apologized for the role Belgian government authorities played in deaths of 28,902 Belgian Jews during the Holocaust. That year, Belgium opened its first Holocaust museum. Somber reminders of the Nazi acts are displayed in a small former prison camp, called Fort Breendonk (shown above) near Antwerp. From this fort, thousands of Jews were registered and deported to German camps.

North African origins. Officially, they account for at least 6 percent of the population, and make up 25 percent of the residents of Brussels. There are thought to be more than 350 mosques, with the main mosque in Brussels forming the center of the Islamic faith in Belgium. This is an active mosque, with a school and many other activities related to Islam.

Several Protestant faiths in Belgium have small followings. The main Protestant churches include the Belgian Evangelical Lutheran, various foreign and Free Churches, and sects like the Jehovah's Witnesses. The Protestant religion in Belgium often reflects a strong Dutch or American influence.

The Jewish population in Belgium is small, around thirty thousand. This is only half its size before World War II. Today Jews largely live in Brussels and, more visibly, in Antwerp. The Jewish community includes Orthodox, Conservative, and Reformed congregations.

In the quiet, green Ardennes forests, the Hare Krishna sect runs its own center of faith and learning. Its faith is based on Hindu scriptures, and its robed followers can be seen occasionally in the cities selling leaflets. The country also has small Buddhist centers following both Thai and Tibetan traditions. There is a small Sikh community in the Flemish sugar-processing city of Tienen.

As in many developed countries, it is not uncommon for some Belgians to consider themselves agnostic or secular humanists, focusing on ethics rather than religion as a philosophical starting point.

INTERNET LINKS

www.timesofisrael.com/divided-belgium-finally-admits-holocaust-complicity
This article takes an interesting look at Belgium's role in the Holocaust.

www.thevoiceleuven.be/evolving-landscape-of-religious-beliefs-in-belgium
This article takes a look at the demographics of religious practice in Belgium.

LANGUAGE

A newstand in Brussels offers newspapers in both French and Flemish.

9

DO YOU SPEAK BELGIAN? OF course not. No one in Belgium speaks it either because there is no such language as Belgian. The country is linguistically split between the Flemish (Flemish speakers) in the north and the Francophones (French speakers) in the south. There is also a small German-speaking minority in eastern Belgium, near the German border.

THE LANGUAGE BARRIER

Long before the modern country of Belgium was created, this small area of Europe was already divided between the two language groups. Frankish tribes speaking a Germanic language settled in the north of the country, while Celts fled to the south, where their language was latinized as they were incorporated into the Roman Empire. The language division continues to this day. Language and politics have always been inextricably linked in Belgium. At different times, each community has tried to force its language on the other, always resulting in trouble and much conflict.

When the Burgundian nobles rose to power, French became the language of the court and, therefore, of government and power. During the Dutch Revolt, Flanders tried to break away from Spanish-

In 2014, the most popular names for girl babies in Flanders were Emma, Louise Elise, Olivia, and Lina; for boys, Louis, Lucas, Arthur, Adam, and Noah. In Wallonia, the girls' names were Léa, Lucie, Chloé, Zoé, and Emma; for boys, Hugo, Louis, Gabriel, Arthur, and Nathan. In Brussels, the popular names reflect the influence of immigrants, with Nour, Yasmine, Malak (girls), and Mohamed, Imran, Amir, and Youssef all making the top ten for each sex.

Flemish demonstrators protest against the use of French during a city council meeting in Wezembeekoppem, a suburb of Brussels.

Catholic control along with fellow Dutch-speaking Holland, but was unsuccessful. Three centuries later, when Belgium briefly joined the Netherlands, William I attempted to impose Dutch as the official language on all the Belgians. It proved to be a bad mistake that ended in general rebellion.

A new constitution, signed in 1831, promised linguistic equality, but in practice it was a great advantage to speak French. Not only did French speakers have an economic advantage, the language was also thought of as being more refined. On the contrary, Flemish was considered the language of farmers and laborers. As a result, many middle-class people of Flemish background chose to speak French to gain social advantages. This trend was reflected in the education system, as all lessons above primary level were conducted in French.

The revival of Flemish was stimulated by Hendrik Conscience and his inspiring book *The Lion of Flanders*, which was published in 1838. It demonstrated that Flemish could be a powerful literary language and it launched the campaign for *taalvrijheid* (TAAHL-vreye-heyet), meaning the freedom of language and the right to use Flemish in official dealings and education. Laws passed in 1898 gave both languages equal status. Nevertheless, as the country industrialized, much of Belgium's economic activity was based in French-speaking Wallonia, adding yet more power to the French part of the country.

Until quite recently, French was the main language of commerce, politics, and management. This meant also that a person usually had to speak French to get the best jobs, even if he or she lived in the Flemish part of the country.

The German occupation of Belgium in 1940 triggered a few Flemish groups to campaign for a separate country under German protection, provoking considerable anti-Flemish feelings after the war. At that time, Belgium was forming far closer political links to France.

The 1960s brought the language question back as a prime issue. An official language frontier was formed in 1962, but the Flemish, believing they were still at a disadvantage, became more determined and occasionally violent in their protests. In 1968 students in the Flemish city of Leuven marched to demand that more classes be given in Flemish rather than French at the country's top university. The marches escalated into riots and eventually, the Francophone part of the university separated and moved to Wallonia.

To resolve the never-ending linguistic problems, Belgium decided to form French, Flemish, and German communities to oversee cultural affairs within their regions. The different language regions acquired considerable autonomy from the central government and many of the past prejudices have now been addressed.

Still, language remains a major issue in Belgium today, and some people even think the language question could eventually split the nation into two. The Flemish daily newspaper *De Standaard* predicted, "It may take a decade, or a generation, but the Belgium state is dissolving itself." Flanders seems increasingly prepared for such an outcome; many of its inhabitants consider themselves Flemish rather than Belgian. In Wallonia, the French-speaking citizens still think of themselves as Belgian but are starting to realize that the country might indeed be split one day. If there were a split, a big dilemma would arise as the country wonders what to do with bilingual Brussels. There, a majority of people speak French, but the city is surrounded by Flanders.

SPOKEN AND WRITTEN LANGUAGES

For all practical purposes, written Flemish is the same as Dutch (Nederlands), the West Germanic language spoken in the Netherlands. But spoken Flemish has several very strong dialects that even the Dutch or other Flemish speakers can find relatively difficult to understand. One interesting difference is that the Dutch have adopted more English and French words into their vocabulary, particularly for technical subjects. In contrast, Flemish tends to create more distinctively Dutch terms to avoid incorporating French words.

Correct Belgian French is about as close to France's French as British English is to American English. To French ears, Belgian French produces a

somewhat comical, throaty sound, while most Belgians find the sound of Parisian French painfully arrogant. However, the two forms of French are mutually intelligible, and Belgians happily watch a considerable quantity of television programs from France. French people find it harder to understand Belgian Francophones, especially if they start to add words from the Walloon dialect.

Brussels is in a unique position. Officially it is a bilingual city, which means that city bureaucrats are expected to be fluent in both Flemish and French. In practice, French or even English is much more widely understood in the city than Flemish. Some Brussels residents speak a blend of French and Flemish known as Bruxellois, the most marked form of which is called Marollien. This mix includes words from Spanish and Yiddish.

This map shows the general distribution of languages in Belgium. The orange section denotes Flemish speakers, the red is the French-speaking section, the green marks the German section, and the crosshatched area is the multilingual Brussels region.

ACCENTS AND DIALECTS

Historically, Belgium was a collection of city-states, resulting in the wide range of local accents and dialects that vary not only from province to province but also from town to town and sometimes even from village to village. Belgians can easily tell where someone comes from by his or her accent and dialect. Some accents and dialects are very distinctive and very hard to understand.

In Flanders the strongest accents are those of Limburg, Aalst, and Ostend. Some Flemish speakers find them difficult to understand. In Wallonia the Liège and Namur accents are also quite distinct and are often used for comic effect when telling jokes. The accents remain an active part of Belgian culture, although some of the most extreme versions are now dying out.

In Wallonia a series of local French dialects of Latin origin and influenced by the Celtic and Germanic languages are collectively known as Walloon. The three main forms of Walloon are almost mutually unintelligible and French speakers need a translator to understand them. All Walloon speakers, though, also understand Belgian French and can speak it, too, albeit often with a very heavy accent. Walloon usage is diminishing, but the language is still used in folkloric events and dialect-based literature and drama.

LANGUAGE AND DAILY LIFE

The language split has many practical implications for Belgian life. There are separate television and radio stations broadcasting in Flemish, French, and German. Newspapers address the different communities in their respective languages. So do ministers and other public figures during official functions. Belgian hospitals, schools, and police forces use one of the three languages, depending on their location in the country.

Belgian road signs can be very confusing for foreigners. That is because many town names are very different in French and Flemish. Things are easy enough in Brussels because road signs are bilingual. In Wallonia, however, directions on signposts are in French, even for Flemish towns. So to head for the town of Kortrijk, for example, a traveller needs to watch for signs to Courtrai. Similarly, signs in Flanders are in Flemish even for Francophone towns. A sign

A tourist signpost in Brussels shows destinations in both French (*top*) and Flemish.

NAMES

At first glance, Belgian last names appear to be clues to the part of the country people come from. It is a reasonable guess that anybody with a name like van Damme or De Wilde is from the northern, Flemish part of the country. Similarly, Delvaux and Lefèvre suggest a Walloon origin. However, there have been centuries of mixing and intermingling between the communities, so in reality, it is almost impossible to accurately associate someone's name with his or her origin. Common last names in Belgium include Janssens, Vermeulen, Lemaitre, Peeters, Bruyne, Dupont, and Roelants. Multibarreled French last names, especially those including the term de *(of) tend to suggest an aristocratic background.*

It is usual for Belgian children of Christian families to be given three names, although only the first will generally be used. In Wallonia, middle names typically include Ghislain (for boys) or Ghislaine (for girls), after the seventh-century Belgian saint, along with the names of the child's godfather or godmother. Most Christian names have both a Flemish version and a French version. For example, Jan and Piet in Flemish translate to Jean and Pierre in French. However, these are not translated in daily life. The versions are interchangeably used only for the names of saints, churches, and royalty.

In recent years television and popular public figures also have a considerable influence on new names, and there is a growing tendency to use anglicized or non-European names for the sake of originality.

pointing to Bergen will lead you to the city of Mons. Some names are easy to identify in either language: Ath is Aat; Lier is Lierre; and Enghien is Edingen. However, some are very different indeed: Liège is Luik; Ronse is Renaix; Jodoigne is Geldenaken; and Jezus-Eik is Notre-Dame-au-Bois! The problem even extends to towns in neighboring countries: Lille in French is called Rijsel in Flemish, while Aachen in Germany is called Aix-la-Chapelle in French.

The language question seldom causes serious problems between individuals on a personal level. However, tensions are high in Flemish towns like Overrijse on the Brussels periphery, where Flemish people fear being swamped by non-Flemish speakers who have been moving into the area in recent decades. In certain places such as Flemish communes, local councils have demanded that people pass a Flemish language test before being allowed to buy land. This has been challenged as a violation of international human rights standards.

THE BELGIAN POLYGLOTS

As a small multilingual country, it is natural for Belgians to speak a second or third language or even more. All children are required to learn a second national language. German and English are the most popular third languages. English is important as a language of advanced study, and as Germany is both a close neighbor and a major trading partner, German is an important language of commerce. Generally, the Flemish seem open to learning another language. They are certainly more likely to speak French than a person from Wallonia is to speak Flemish. In Flanders, learning English is also helped by having television programs that are subtitled rather than dubbed in English. In Wallonia, most programs are dubbed into French.

INTERNET LINKS

belgium.beertourism.com/about-belgium/language-matters
This site gives a good overview of the language situation in Belgium.

www.theguardian.com/world/2010/may/09/belgium-flanders-wallonia-french-dutch
This is a good article about the language problems in Belgium.

www.omniglot.com
Omniglot offers good introductions to Dutch, Flemish, French, German, and Walloon.

ARTS

Street musicians in Brussels perform at a presentation of a new costume to the famous statue Mannekin Pis.

10

"Art evokes the mystery without which the world would not exist."
—René Magritte (1898-1967), Belgian surrealist artist

A S IS SO OFTEN THE CASE WHEN IT comes to Belgium, the history of its arts and culture proceeds along two or more separate tracks. The work of most Belgian artists is influenced and determined by their Francophone, Flemish, or even Walloon backgrounds. Moreover, many of the greatest Belgian artists worked long before the founding of the nation itself.

Early in the last century, the work of artists such as the painter James Ensor and the composer César Franck started to inspire a national feeling, sometimes called La Belgitude. There was also a generation of writers who wrote in French but whose stories drew from the history and culture of Flanders. As the language question became more important, it started to have a major influence in the world of art. In the 1960s, the formation of separate ministries of education and culture widened the division between the Walloon and Flemish cultures.

Today, French-speaking Belgians tend to follow the trends of France. This is reflected in the books they read, the plays they watch, and the music they listen to. Many of Belgium's best French-speaking artists have moved to France, in particular Paris, where they find the art scene more stimulating. The Flemish-speaking community has always appeared more interested in forging its own cultural identity and is not particularly influenced by events in the Netherlands. Nevertheless, the proximity of the German and, notably, Anglo-Saxon cultures does lead to their influence on Flemish culture.

BELGIUM'S RICH CULTURAL PAST

Belgium has a rich artistic legacy. Until the fourteenth century, almost all art was commissioned by the church or nobility, and most paintings were either portraits or religious scenes, painted onto panels to decorate the altars in churches. As Flemish towns like Bruges developed, rich folk were increasingly able to commission portraits for themselves. Perhaps the most famous Flemish masters were the brothers Jan and Hubert van Eyck, who developed new techniques of oil painting that allowed them to add far more detail to their works than had been possible before.

Since cameras were not invented yet, ordinary folks started asking artists to include their homes and possessions in their portraits. Thus the art of landscape painting started to develop, initially as background. The van Eycks still worked on religious images and their *Adoration of the Lamb* (an altarpiece) is considered to be the greatest masterpiece of this period.

The second half of the fifteenth century is best remembered for the work of the Flemish painter Hans Memling. He settled in Bruges in 1465 and, despite the fact that the economy of the city was declining, managed to win important commissions. His paintings are admired for their beautiful detail.

The simmering religious revolution at the start of the sixteenth-century led several Flemish painters to follow the imaginative style of Dutch master Hieronymus Bosch (1450—1516). Bosch painted scenes of the afterlife with bizarre creatures inflicting terrible punishments on sinners. His work was really a form of surrealism, although it was to be several more centuries before that term would be first used.

The last great Flemish master of this period was Pieter Bruegel the Elder (1525—1569). He covered a wider range of subjects, including group portraits, landscapes, and still life. His pictures give an excellent idea of what life was like during this period. *Hunters in the Snow* (1565), one of his most beloved paintings, portrays a winter landscape in a small Flemish village. His famous painting *The Numbering of Bethlehem* shows Joseph and Mary on their donkey arriving at the inn, with the scene set in sixteenth-century Flanders. Most of his canvases also contained strong social commentaries, which appealed to middle-class art buyers.

Within a generation, however, everything changed. While the newly independent Netherlands continued to develop secular art, encouraging the brooding genius of Rembrandt, the Dutch Revolts left Belgium suffering a drastic economic collapse. The only rich sponsor for art was the Catholic

Hunters in the Snow is one of the most famous paintings by Pieter Bruegel the Elder.

Church. This led foremost seventeenth-century Flemish masters like Peter Paul Rubens to concentrate on producing vast canvases of angels and cherubs effectively glorifying the power and might of the church. Like many artists of the time, Rubens trained in Italy and produced an astonishing amount of work, ranging from giant altarpieces to portraits. Toward the end of his life Rubens retired to the countryside, where he painted landscapes for the first time.

Tapestry weaving flourished in the fifteenth and sixteenth centuries, and Belgium's large tapestries were considered to be the best in the world; they hung in palaces, churches, and noble homes all over Europe. The tapestries illustrated scenes from mythology, hunting, tales of chivalry, or Bible stories. The town of Oudenaarde specialized in "green" tapestries using patterns of leaves and plants.

Designs for tapestries were created by the best artists, and even Rubens once worked on a special design for the Vatican. Once the design was drawn, teams of five or six workers did the weaving, using colored yarns made from wool or silk. Gold and silver yarns were also used.

Belgian tapestries can be seen in museums around the country, and a special tapestry museum is located in Tournai (Doornik). The Royal Tapestry Manufacturers in Mechelen and some individual artists still keep the old skills alive.

MODERN PAINTERS

At the end of the nineteenth century the enigmatic Symbolist movement inspired painters such as Léon Spilliaert and the brilliant Fernand Khnopff, whose figures often appear in part-human, part-animal forms. Another very original painter was James Ensor, whose use of light, masks, and hybrid forms inspired many later artists.

The Surrealist movement of the 1920s had the strongest influence on modern Belgian painting, producing two world-famous modern painters, René Magritte and Paul Delvaux. Delvaux was fascinated by trains and the Brussels trams. These often appear in his work as dark and sinister objects. Motionless nude figures with empty eyes are a common motif throughout Delvaux's work.

ARCHITECTURE

As well as religious masterpieces, the genius of medieval Belgian architecture is most apparent in the merchants' houses of Bruges and in fabulous soaring bell towers and trading halls that are found all across the country. These were a visible symbol of a town's wealth and independence and superb examples remain in Bruges, Saint Truiden, Lier, Ghent, and many other towns.

Belgian architecture came into its own again in the early twentieth century, taking inspiration from the Art Nouveau movement. The totally new style used fluid spiral lines and natural curls, and was influenced by the Japanese, Celtic, and Turkish arts and the observation of nature. The strong sense for detail and beauty turned the movement into a highly decorative style. With architects Victor Horta and Henry van de Velde, Brussels once boasted the most beautiful Art Nouveau treasures in Europe. Tragically, careless monument protection policy and the demolition ball that tore through most cities in the 1960s and 1970s mean that relatively little of this heritage has survived.

THE STRANGE, LONELY WORLD OF RENÉ MAGRITTE

The paintings of René Magritte are full of fascinating and strange ideas that challenge the viewer's perceptions of reality. His images are clear and simple but provoke unsettling thoughts and feelings of alienation. Rocks float, leaves turn into trees, trees into birds, and a gray mountainside is, at the same time, a great eagle. One of the most famous canvases from his early period, The Treachery of Images *(1929), is a simple painting of a pipe, beneath which is written* Ceci n'est pas une pipe *("This is not a pipe").*

*One of Magritte's favorite motifs was a man in a bowler hat, which he himself often wore. In these paintings, the man's face is obscured by a green apple (*The Son of Man, *1946) or a dove (*Man in a Bowler Hat, *1964), or expressionless men in bowler hats and black suits rain down on a lifeless city (*Golconda, *1953). Other common*

motifs in his work include eyes, clouds, and figures with draped faces.

Magritte spent most of his life living quietly in Brussels. His work enjoyed great popular success in the 1960s, late in his life, and it continues to be referenced frequently in popular culture today. The Son of Man, *for example, is probably his best-known painting, familiar even to people who have little knowledge of art or Magritte himself.*

The Magritte Museum in Brussels, which displays some two hundred of his works, opened in 2009 next to the Royal Museums of Fine Arts of Belgium. Other works by Magritte are on exhibit in museums worldwide.

MUSIC

Belgium might not exist if it were not for opera. The revolution of 1830, from which Belgium was ultimately created, started when Francophone Belgians became stirred up by nationalist sentiment in an 1830 production of Daniel Auber's La Muette de Portici at Théâtre de la Monnaie, the Brussels opera house. The rest is history.

As early as the fifteenth century, Belgium was famous for its choirs, which sang in four-part harmony. Belgian composers became famous in the princely churches and chapels of Rome, Milan, and Munich, and musicians came from all over Europe hoping to learn the secrets of the Flemish sound. As the Baroque style developed at the end of the sixteenth century, these Flemish musicians lost favor.

Belgian music took on a new life in the nineteenth century with composer César Franck (1822—1890). He was born in Liège, although he spent most of his musical career in Paris, where he worked as an organist and a professor at the Paris Conservatory. Franck produced a number of impressive compositions for piano, organ, and orchestra, as well as chamber music and religious oratorios. His use of a subtle counterpoint form gained him recognition as a modernizer of French music and one of the great composers of his time. His home city has opened a conservatory of music in his honor.

Peter Benoit (1834—1901) was a Flemish composer who produced important works for piano, orchestra, operas, and choruses. His masterpiece is often considered to be the oratorio *Lucifer* (1866). Benoit was passionate about creating a distinctively Flemish style of music that differed from the well-known French and German schools of the time. In 1867, he founded and directed the Flemish School of Music in Antwerp, which later became the Royal Flemish Conservatory. Under Benoit's influence, other Flemish music schools in Brussels and Ghent flourished.

Belgium does a great deal to encourage musicians. There are several major national competitions, as well as important international music festivals that include classical, jazz, and popular music. The world-reputed International Queen Elizabeth Contest focuses on performances by pianists, violinists, and vocalists and is held in alternating years. It attracts contestants from around the globe.

Belgians have a very international taste in pop music, with a strong preference for classic rock, blues, and a variety of new-age sounds. Francophone Belgians are keen followers of French pop, rap, and chanson singers, and are immensely proud that Jaques Brel, one of France's

SAX INVENTS THE SAX

Born in 1814, Adolphe Sax worked in his father's musical instruments workshop in Dinant making flutes and clarinets. He was only twenty-six when he invented his first instrument, a brass tube fitted with a single reed. Its sound was similar to a clarinet but deeper and mellower. Inspired, Sax went on to make a series of new instruments that he called "saxhorns," which combined the power of brass instruments with the expressiveness of woodwinds.

In 1946, Sax took out a patent on his new "saxophone," which was a combination of a clarinet and an ophicleide, an older, keyed brass instrument. As the world of music was very conservative, Sax had trouble persuading people to take his new instrument seriously. It didn't help that he was thought to have a difficult personality. However, once the saxophone was accepted by military marching bands, it slowly grew in popularity.

While the saxophone never did become a symphonic instrument, it found a special place in jazz and rock bands. Sax's other instruments never quite caught on but played a role in the development of similar new horns. His saxotromba, saxhorn, and saxtuba would later be tweaked by other inventors and appear as the flugelhorn, the euphonium, and the bass tuba.

greatest all-time vocal legends, was in fact Belgian. Flanders produces a certain amount of polka-oompah music, but top Flemish groups tend to sing in English.

CINEMA

Belgian cinema has enjoyed a certain renown for tackling weighty issues. Many films are more thought-provoking than entertaining. André Delvaux, probably Belgium's most famous filmmaker, directed his films in both Flemish

Jean-Claude Van Damme is best known for martial arts action films.

and French, and adapted novels of Flemish and Belgian-French origin. Stijn Coninx was nominated for an Oscar in 1993 for his social drama *Daens*, filmed in Flemish. Of Francophone filmmakers, Belgium's most successful are the brothers Luc and Jean-Pierre Dardenne. They achieved the extremely rare accolade of winning the Cannes Palme d'Or three times with *Rosetta* (1999), *L'Enfant* (2005), and *Deux Jours, Une Nuit* (*Two Days, One Night*) in 2014. Chantal Akerman's French-language films are also much admired. In 2012, the Flemish film *Rundskop* (*Bullhead*) directed by Michaël R. Roskam, was nominated for the Academy Award for Best Foreign Film; and in 2013, another Belgian film, *The Broken Circle Breakdown* directed by Felix Van Groeningen, also set in Flanders, took that honor.

Among filmgoers rather than critics, one of the most popular Belgian films is Jaco van Dormael's *Le Huitième Jour* (*The Eighth Day*, 1996) about a young man with Down syndrome. Van Dormael went on to direct the 2009 English-language film *Mr. Nobody*, which won wide critical acclaim. Since its original release, the movie has gone on to become a cult film, noted for its characterization, philosophy, cinematography, and soundtrack. Van Dormael presented his fourth feature film, *Le Tout Nouveau Testament* (*The Brand New Testament*) at the Cannes Film Festival in 2015 to critical praise.

Belgium itself also annually hosts several film festivals, the most important of which are the Flanders International Film Festival in Ghent and the Brussels International Festival of Fantasy Film. Belgium's most internationally famous film star is the martial arts actor Jean-Claude Van Damme. Nicknamed "Muscles from Brussels," Van Damme is probably the most instantly recognized Belgian face in Asia and the United States. Few people realize that screen idol Audrey Hepburn was born in Brussels.

Second only to Japan, Belgium is the home of cartoon, or comic, books. These are considered works of art and are by no means exclusive to children. The most internationally famous character is Tintin, the young reporter, with his dog, Snowy, and his friend, Captain Haddock. Created by cartoonist Hergé, shown at right, Tintin first appeared in the 1929 adventure Tintin in the Land of the Soviets. *Since then his adventures have taken him all over the world and even to the moon. The Tintin series was one of the most popular European comics of the twentieth century.*

Other famous Belgian cartoons include Spirou, Marsupilami, and Lucky Luke. Spirou is a hotel bellboy who has a series of exciting and comical adventures. Lucky Luke is a cowboy with a faithful horse, Jolly Jumper, and Marsupilami is a strange spotted animal from outer space.

Cartoon and animation films have also been successful in the Belgian and international film industries. The rather earthy but very humorous films by Brussels's humorist Picha have been screened all over the world, and Raoul Servais and Nicole van Goethem, from Ghent and Antwerp, respectively, have won several international awards.

FAMOUS LACE MAKING

Lace making is a classic Belgian craft. The tradition is especially strong in Brussels and the surrounding Brabant countryside. Lace first became popular in the sixteenth century when rich men and women wore it to decorate their clothing and to flaunt their wealth.

Brussels lace was particularly prized, as it was finely made and used interesting designs. At the height of the fashion for lace in the seventeenth

MANNEKEN PIS

Most big cities in the world are adorned with outdoor statues, usually of great heroes portrayed in a grand, idealized fashion. Brussels has those as well, but its best known statue is Manneken Pis, a small bronze sculpture of a little boy. It has become the semiofficial symbol of Brussels, and it fits well with the citizens' gentle, self-mocking humor.

Nobody really knows why the statue was built, but there are numerous far-fetched tales of its origin. One version is that an unknown boy made the mistake of relieving himself outside a witch's house. The angry witch responded by turning him into a statue. In another story the statue was put up by grateful parents whose son was found on this spot after wandering off during a busy carnival. More common than either of those is the tale of a little boy who spotted a fire during his excursion to the outhouse one evening. By raising the alarm, he saved the city from being burned down.

Manneken Pis was originally a stone statue, carved by Jérôme Duquesnoy in 1619. It was replaced by a bronze version in 1817. Both suffered frequent thefts by student pranksters and by invading armies. Troops of Louis XV stole one in 1747 and dumped it in the street. The French king apologized by sending a fine set of clothes to "dress" him. Since then, Manneken Pis's wardrobe has grown to more than 650 garments. He often wears uniforms or national costumes depending on sponsors and special occasions.

and eighteenth centuries, the industry employed thousands of women, giving them an important source of income.

The economic importance of lace making became quite a political issue. At one point the British government became worried about how much money was being spent on Belgian lace, and they tried to ban its import. Emperor Philip II of Belgium sought to prevent girls over the age of twelve from working in the industry. It was attracting so many of them that it had become difficult to find anybody willing to work as servants. Neither ruler had much success with these campaigns. Eventually wearing lace simply went out of fashion.

Today tourism and a growing interest in the past have revived lace making, and many Belgian women have started learning and practicing the art, both as a hobby and as a source of extra income. Most of the lace, usually used for tablecloths and blouses, finds its way to tourist shops in Bruges and Brussels. Because of the work involved and the high cost of labor in Belgium, handmade lace is expensive. Machine-made lace is far more affordable.

INTERNET LINKS

www.independent.co.uk/arts-entertainment/art/features/smoke-and-mirrors-the-surreal-life-and-work-of-ren-magritte-2295262.html
This article is an engaging look at the life and work of René Magritte.

www.metmuseum.org/toah/hd/brue/hd_brue.htm
This section from the Metropolitan Museum of Art focuses on the Antwerp painter Pieter Bruegel.

www.metmuseum.org/toah/hd/eyck/hd_eyck.htm
The life and works of Jan van Eyck are well explained here, with many links.

www.pri.org/stories/2013-12-03/meet-dangerous-belgian-who-invented-sax
This story about Adolphe Sax is also available in audio.

www.smurf.com/en/history
The official Smurfs site has a section on Peyo.

The Smurfs, the little blue elf-like creatures, began life in 1958 as a comic strip by the Belgian cartoon artist Peyo (Pierre Cilluford). The Smurfs were already generating international merchandising success when the US animation studio Hanna-Barbera created the Saturday morning cartoon series The Smurfs in 1981. Peyo died in 1992, but his little characters live on, most recently in the 2011 movie The Smurfs.

LEISURE

A sunny day in Ghent brings people outside to relax.

11

In celebration of the 2014 FIFA (soccer) World Cup event; the famous Manneken Pis statue in Brussels was dressed in a miniature version of the new Belgian soccer team uniform in the national colors of black, yellow, and red.

MOST BELGIANS HAVE THE TIME and money to enjoy some leisure. By law, Belgian workers are granted a minimum of twenty days of paid vacation and ten days of paid holidays. A standard workweek is between thirty-five and thirty-nine hours, and more than that counts as overtime.

GETTING OUTDOORS

Belgians are great sun worshippers. Because the weather tends to be gray and cold much of the time, people like to head outdoors whenever it is sunny and warm, and barbecues are extremely popular among those with backyards of their own.

Belgians love to catch up with each other over a drink at the local café or pub, where time is also spent listening to popular music or playing games. Certain cafés offer card and board games, chess, and variants of billiards and pool. Some offer appealing outdoor terraces.

Art lovers enjoy an extensive selection of museums and art galleries throughout the country, and great art exhibitions are organized in the major cities. During special exhibitions and carnivals, the Belgian railway company often offers special travel packages.

BELGIAN SHEEPDOGS

Big, strong sheepdogs were originally bred to work on farms, but today many are popular with police forces and among dog lovers globally. Northern Europe is famous for the Alsatian and German shepherd dogs, but Belgium has four highly prized breeds of its own. The most lovable are the Tervuren with its luxuriant, long-haired mahogany coat, and the black Groenendael. They make good family pets. The Laekenois has stiffer, somewhat curly hair that makes it look a little disheveled. The famous Malinois has a short, glossy coat and a dark face. Malinois can be especially aggressive and are often used in police work. However, their unpredictable temperaments make them hard to control as family pets.

HOBBIES AND PETS

Belgians enjoy a whole range of hobbies. The bigger cities have shops catering to the needs of stamp collectors, model makers, and toy-train collectors, as well as numerous pet stores. Many Belgians are keen collectors who like hunting in antiques dealers' shops and at numerous outdoor markets, notably in Brussels's Sablon area and in Tongeren on Sundays.

Many towns also have sports clubs, cultural circles, choirs, amateur theater groups, brass bands, youth clubs, senior citizens' clubs, and political groups. Even small towns generally have a cultural center with occasional performances, travel lectures, and concerts. Gardening is a very popular pastime for people living in suburbs or villages.

Many Belgians have a soft spot for pets, with cats, dogs, and birds being the favorites. Cities are quite dog friendly, and many restaurants allow dogs in to sit by their person's table. However, Belgians haven't developed the habit of picking up after their dogs, as the city streets often prove.

VACATIONS

During short vacations and weekends, the population is quick to rush off to the sandy North Sea beaches or to go hiking and skiing in the hilly Ardennes. There are no permanent ski resorts because the snow is too unpredictable, but cross-country enthusiasts abound.

Belgium has its own amusement and theme parks, which include water parks, zoos, and safari parks. It is possible to boat calmly along Belgium's extensive canal system and inland waterways, ride old steam trains, or explore caves in the Ardennes.

Longer vacations are more likely to be taken abroad, not just because there is a better chance of enjoying sunshine but also because it often works out cheaper than vacationing at the Belgian coast. The most popular foreign getaway destinations are France, Spain, Turkey, Greece, Egypt, and Tunisia.

TELEVISION AND INTERNET

Television broadcasting in Flanders is completely separate from that in Wallonia. Belgium has one of the most extensive systems of cable television in the world. With more than 90 percent of its households having access to cable channels, the average family receives not just Belgian programming but also a selection of productions from other nations, typically France, the Netherlands, the United Kingdom, Germany, Portugal, Italy, and Spain, along with European CNN, MTV, and Euro News channels. However, despite these choices, most cable operators in Wallonia do not offer more than one Flemish channel. Similarly, in Flanders a viewer is as likely to obtain broadcasting from France in French as from Wallonia.

Being a small nation with a limited audience means that Belgian television cannot afford to produce many television dramas of its own and therefore must import shows from other countries. The French region naturally favors programs made in France, but both areas telecast programs from Britain and the United States. In Flemish areas, these will generally be shown in English with subtitles. In Wallonia, the programs are usually dubbed into French. Radio is still very popular. People typically tune in to their favorite station in the mornings, and especially when driving, if only for warnings about traffic delays and police speed checks. It is not at all unusual to have the radio playing quietly in factories and cafés. There are dozens of radio stations divided by language, region, and theme. Specialist stations cater to minority groups, including Italian and Turkish speakers.

Internet use is high in Belgium. In 2015, some 81 to 83 percent of Belgians were online, which is slightly higher than the European Union average of 78.5 percent. For context, the US average was 87.4 percent and the world average was 42.1 percent. In 2013, 47.1 percent of Belgians were Facebook subscribers.

CYCLING

Cycling is the national sport of Belgium. There is a strong network of clubs where members train together for competitions. The Tour of Belgium is considered one of the top events on the professional cycling calendar. However, nothing in the sport compares with the excitement of the Tour de France, which often passes through Belgium at some stage to let Belgian racing fans enjoy the spectacle. Belgian cyclists have a good record in the event—one of the most famous cyclists of all time is Belgian Eddy Merckx (b. 1945), who won the Tour de France five times.

A cycling race passes through Lierde, in the hilly region of the Flemish Ardennes.

Thousands of locals go cycling in the countryside every weekend, and they view this as much of a social occasion as a sporting competition. In Flanders many locals keep an old "boneshaker" for making short trips around town, and there are considerable networks of cycle paths. Several touring circuits have been set up around the country, notably the Vlaanderen route, which covers a distance of 398 miles (640 km).

Most of Belgium is flat, which makes cycling easy and popular. However, especially in Wallonia, cycling on public roads can be hazardous due to inconsiderate driving.

SOCCER

Extremely popular with Belgian men, soccer is played at all levels and by all age groups. In the villages, the soccer team is often an important part of the local social life. Dances and other events organized by the community help to raise a little money to run the team.

The first official international soccer match in continental Europe was held in Belgium in 1904. In the history of the national team, Bernard Voorhoof and Paul Van Himst are the highest-scoring Belgium players, with a tally of thirty goals each.

Most of Belgium's home matches are played at the King Baudouin Stadium in Brussels. In May 2013, it was announced that King Baudouin Stadium would be replaced by a new one, to be called the Eurostadium, which is set to be completed in 2019. In September 2014, the Union of European Football Associations (UEFA) named Brussels as one of the thirteen host cities for the 2020 European championship, with its new stadium hosting four games.

Belgium hasn't always performed well on the international stage, but since 2012, a new "golden age" has emerged under guidance of manager Marc Wilmots. The team reached the 2014 World Cup quarter-finals and qualified for Euro 2016. It topped the FIFA World Rankings for the first time in November 2015. FIFA is the world governing body of professional soccer.

Belgium's national team, nicknamed the Red Devils, is now considered to be one of the few positive symbols of a unified Belgium and is supported by Flemish and Francophone Belgians alike.

Sven Kums of Ghent plays in a UEFA Champions League match in December 2015.

PIGEON RACING

Belgium, along with the north of England, can claim to be the founder and home of pigeon racing. Many special species of racing pigeons have been bred around Antwerp, and Belgium founded the international body that governs the sport.

Pigeon racing is particularly strong in the rural regions and is very much a male–dominated activity. Although it is seen mostly as an activity for older people, many men teach the sport to their sons. The duivenmelker *(DEUY-vuhn-mehl-kuhr), or pigeon racer, plans the breeding program in the hope of producing champions, trains pigeons for the big events, and bets on them as well.*

Races are governed by strict rules. The pigeons are handed over to the race officials in the hometown and taken away to be released together. Races generally start over short distances and get longer as the season progresses. By the end of a racing year, the birds might be taken as far as southern France before being released to find their way back. They usually fly at 40 miles per hour (64 kilometers per hour) but with a strong wind behind them, they can go much faster.

When the pigeons are due to arrive home, the nervous owner tries to keep everybody in the house quiet, as pigeons may not land if they are alarmed by any noise. As soon as a pigeon lands, a ring is removed from its foot and placed into a special time clock that records the finishing time for the bird. The sealed clock is taken to the club headquarters, where the pigeon racer finds out how his champion bird has performed against its rivals. Half the fun of pigeon racing comes from the social aspect of the competition, and most owners spend the afternoons in discussion with fellow racers.

OTHER SPORTS

The remarkable success of Belgian tennis greats Kim Clijsters and Justine Henin thrust tennis into the forefront of Belgian sporting interest. Professional basketball also has a considerable following, notably in the city of Charleroi. Brussels organizes an annual marathon and has "Roller Days" where sections of town are briefly shut down for a swarm of roller skaters to whiz through.

Motor sports are also popular. The Belgian Formula One Grand Prix Spa-Francorchamps course is frequently said to be the favorite for drivers. Belgium's most famous Formula One stars were Thierry Boutson and Jacky Ickx.

Belgium has more than fifty golf clubs. The Royal Antwerp Club was founded in 1888, making it one of the oldest in the world. Golf was introduced by British workers who came to Belgium in the nineteenth century to help build railways and factories. The French pastime of *pétanque* (peh-TAHNK), a subdued bowling game generally played outdoors, has a fairly strong following in Wallonia.

In 2013, a Chinese businessman paid a world record price of about $400,000 (€310,000) for a Belgian racing pigeon named Bolt (after the Jamaican sprinter and Olympic gold-medal winner Usain Bolt).

INTERNET LINKS

dogtime.com/dog-breeds/belgian-sheepdog
This site gives a good overview of the Belgian shepherd breeds.

www.spa-francorchamps.be/en
This is the site of the Grand Prix de Spa-Francorchamps and includes a history of the track.

www.uefa.com/worldcup/season=2014/teams/team=13
The UEFA site reports the latest information about the Belgium national soccer team.

FESTIVALS

Brightly costumed street performers celebrate Belgian National Day in Brussels.

12

BELGIANS LOVE FESTIVALS! IN both Flanders and Wallonia, there are unique carnivals, parades, and processions. These vibrant celebrations often feature hundreds of people dressed in astonishing costumes. Some of these events correspond to holidays, others are simply regional traditions.

Belgium's national holidays include New Year's Day (January 1), Labor Day (May 1), Easter Monday (dates vary), National Day (July 21), the Assumption (August 15), All Saints' Day (November 1), Armistice Day (November 11), and Christmas Day (December 25). In addition, each linguistic community has a regional holiday.

CHRISTMAS

Christmas is an important celebration in Belgium as it is with most Christian countries. Pretty lights and decorations add character to townscapes. Schools close for a two-week-long vacation, although most workers get only one day's statutory holiday. Belgian children effectively get to enjoy two Christmases. The first set of presents arrives on Saint Nicholas's Day, December 6. Children leave out socks or boots and hope to find them filled by Saint Nicholas, or *Sinterklaas*, the Belgian Santa Claus. It is typical to leave a carrot for Santa's donkey—in Belgium, Santa does not use Rudolf the Red-nosed Reindeer. December 6 is not a holiday, but it is a tradition to eat specially formed

THE PROBLEM OF ZWARTE PIET

When Santa makes holiday appearances in the United States, he often brings along Mrs. Claus, the elves, and the reindeer. In parts of Europe, however, it's customary for good Saint Nick to be accompanied by a rather wicked fellow. In Switzerland, he is Schmutzli *(from* schmutz, *meaning "dirt"), in France, he is* Père Fouttard *(from* fouet, *or "whip"). In Austria and parts of Germany, the* Krampus *is the scary Christmas guy, and in the Netherland and Flanders, Santa's companion is Zwarte Piet, or Black Pete.*

In these guises, the characters all play a similar role. Sometimes terrifying and other times merely mischievous, he is a devilish and usually darker-skinned being who scares children into behaving properly. To be sure, the folkloric character represents the darker side of human nature, but the literal expression of him as dark-skinned has recently raised charges of racism, especially in regards to Black Pete.

In Flanders and the Netherlands, Black Pete is a much beloved character; he traditionally has exaggerated red lips, and wears flamboyant gold earrings. Pete is said to be a Moor (a Spanish person of North African descent) and is often played by a white man in blackface. Pete's job as a companion to Sinterklaas (who is always white) is to amuse children and hand out treats—while keeping an eye out for disobedient kids to carry off to Spain in a sack. Pete is comical, clownish, and to some observers, uncomfortably reminiscent of the demeaning blackface stereotypes that were thought to be so funny in American minstrel shows a century ago.

In recent years, critics have charged that Black Pete is an inappropriate holdover from an earlier, colonial era, but Pete supporters vehemently disagree. Nevertheless, in

2015, the United Nations Committee on the Elimination of Racial Discrimination issued a report stating "the character of Black Pete is sometimes portrayed in a manner that reflects negative stereotypes of people of African descent and is experienced by many people of African descent as a vestige of slavery." The Center for Equal Opportunities and Opposition to Racism, a Belgian government agency, decided that the image of Zwarte Piet is not in violation of the country's anti-discrimination and anti-racism laws. However, it did encourage an open debate and asked that celebrants refrain from representing "the figure of Zwarte Piet as a stupid, inferior, or dangerous black man."

Some people propose explaining Pete's black face as the sooty result of sliding down chimneys. Others suggest changing his skin color to blue or orange, while traditionalists hotly resist any changes at all to the popular childhood character.

speculoos (SPEH-kuh-loohs) (gingerbread cookies) on that day. Saint Nicholas often appears in shopping centers or special festive markets in Belgium, usually accompanied by a man with an artificially blackened face. This mysterious stick-wielding figure is *Zwarte Piet* (Black Pete or Black Peter). It is supposedly Black Pete's job to check that children have been good enough to deserve their presents.

On the evening of Christmas Eve, December 24, family members enjoy a special dinner together. Many families, even those who do not usually attend church, might attend the Midnight Mass on Christmas Eve. Christmas Day is often a time to visit relatives, and lunch is the main meal of the day. On Christmas Day everybody, not just the children, exchanges presents.

NEW YEAR

New Year's Eve has far less tradition attached to it and is simply a time to go out and enjoy oneself. This might mean attending a party or dining at a restaurant. Toward midnight people often gather in the town center to welcome the new year together. Many towns give a spectacular display of fireworks at midnight.

NATIONAL AND COMMUNITY HOLIDAYS

Belgium's National Day is July 21. It celebrates the day King Leopold I took his oath as monarch. There are festivities throughout the country and a military parade in Brussels. Vielesam's blueberry festival is held the same day. It is preceded on the evening before by a remarkable "capture" of the little town by "Macralle witches" who then put on a show in thick Walloon dialect.

Each linguistic community has its own principal holiday. On July 11 the Flemish community celebrates the anniversary of the Battle of the Golden Spurs. The French community day falls on September 27, commemorating the day patriots in Brussels enjoyed a victory over the Dutch in 1830. The German-speaking community celebrates its national day on November 15.

A military band plays during Belgian National Day celebrations in Brussels.

Armistice Day, November 11, is the day in 1918 that World War I came to an end, but the national holiday commemorates those who died in all wars since. The day means more to older people who remember the World Wars. Special services are conducted at the sites of battlefields, and flowers are placed at war monuments. Churches hold memorial services for those who died for their country, and old soldiers proudly don their uniforms again.

CARNIVALS AND OTHER EVENTS

Belgium has some of the world's most fascinating carnivals. Although carnivals traditionally fall on Mardi Gras, the Tuesday before Lent—the forty days before Easter—somewhere in Belgium there is at least one carnival held virtually every weekend from January until Easter itself. In certain towns carnivals are the most important events in the people's year, and various voluntary groups work together to organize street parades. Among the most famous and distinctive is the Laetare Stavelot, held in the Wallonia town of Stavelot on the fourth Saturday of Lent. Its Blancs Moussis, which date to 1502, are white-robed characters wearing long-nosed masks who throw pig bladders at spectators. Another well-known carnival is the one in Binche,

BINCHE, THE CARNIVAL TOWN

The little town of Binche in southern Belgium lives for its carnival, a yearly celebration that can be traced back to the fourteenth century. The key figures are the Gilles (JEEH-luh), clowns wearing wooden clogs and bright, colorful medieval costumes stuffed with straw and decorated with heraldic lions. Bells hang from their belts, jangling as they make a curious shuffling dance to the sound of brass bands and drums. Being a Gille is considered a great honor, which is passed on from father to son.

The carnival has two climaxes. The first occurs at around 11 a.m. when groups of Gilles converge on the central square. They then put on spooky masks before entering the beautiful city hall building. In the afternoon there is a more formal procession. This time the Gilles wear high hats with enormous plumes of ostrich feathers

and throw oranges into the crowd from special baskets. Oranges are sometimes thrown so hard that some Binche residents board up their windows for protection. However, if spectators are hit, it is considered a wondrous, albeit painful, blessing. Throwing oranges back again would be considered extremely offensive. The festival ends with a giant bonfire and considerable public intoxication as everybody drinks beer throughout the day.

on Mardi Gras, featuring the extraordinary Gilles. The day before Mardis Gras the German-speaking town of Eupen celebrates Rose Monday with an especially lively and colorful carnival. The multiday carnival at Aalst has a unique, if rather boisterous, feel to it. It starts on Sunday with a procession of "giants," Monday sees onion-throwing parades, and the celebration ends with the hilarious "dirty aunts" parade, where most of the town's male population dress up in gaudy women's clothing.

EASTER CELEBRATION AND PROCESSIONS

At Easter painted eggs are traditionally hidden in gardens for children to seek out. These days it is also common to send cards to friends and give chocolate eggs as gifts, much as in the United States. At Eastertime, churches see some of the largest congregations of the year. Small towns and villages have their own Easter parades, such as this one in Hakendover. Among the strangest Easter parades is the Procession of Penitents. This occurs on the night of Good Friday in the Walloon town of Lessines. Participants march solemnly around the darkened streets carrying heavy wooden crosses and dressed in cloaks with conical hoods.

The Procession of the Holy Blood is an Ascension Day parade in Bruges. Hundreds of people dressed as Biblical figures march through the streets. At the center of the procession, priests carry a receptacle said to contain drops of Jesus's blood. On Trinity Sunday, Mons's classic Saint Wadru festival culminates with a Procession of the Golden Carriage and a fight between Saint George and the dragon. The Mons Saint George is actually dressed as a seventeenth-century cavalryman rather than a third-century knight. The battle represents the struggle between good and evil, but for spectators the fun is in the attempt to grab a hair from the dragon's long tail.

HISTORICAL PARADES

Some of Belgium's parades and festivals are reenactments of historic events. The most famous celebration in Brussels is the *Ommegang* (OHM-muh-gang) in July, which is modeled on a parade staged before Charles V in 1549. In the evening, more than two thousand of the city's residents dress up in medieval costumes and parade around the city and into the Grand Place. The parade includes horse riders, stilt walkers, jesters, soldiers, aristocrats, and finally the imperial family and their court. Even Manneken Pis, the little boy statue, joins in the celebration and is dressed in a special festival costume.

Bruges's medieval parade, the Procession of the Golden Tree, takes place only once every five years. It is a stylized reenactment of the 1468 wedding of Charles the Bold and Princess Margaret of York.

Ieper (Ypres) is famous for the Festival of Cats, which dates back to the Middle Ages and the belief that cats were associated with the devil. To disprove this idea, Count Baudouin had all the cats taken to the tower of the town hall and thrown off to show they were not immortal. This bloody and bizarre spectacle went on until the nineteenth century. Today only soft toys are thrown from the tower. The festival also has a magnificent parade with bands, medieval costumes, and, of course, giant cats.

In August, giant figures parade through the town of Ath. With their blue, white, and red costumes, the huge figures look like Napoleon's soldiers. The highlight is a reenactment of the fight between David and Goliath.

INTERNET LINKS

www.carnavaldebinche.be/home-eng.html
The Carnival of Binche site has lots of information and photo galleries.

www.expatica.com/be/about/culture-history/Festivals-in-Belgium_104668.html
This listing of Top Belgian Festivals is regularly updated.

www.laetare-stavelot.be/en
This site of the Stavelot festival has some wonderful photos.

www.nytimes.com/2013/12/05/opinion/why-the-dutch-love-black-pete.html
This opinion piece offers insight into the Christmas character Black Pete.

www.unesco.org/culture/ich/en/state/belgium-BE?info=elements-on-the-lists
The UNESCO site lists the elements of Intangible Cultural Heritage for Belgium, with links.

FOOD

A window display of Belgian waffles tempts hungry passers-by in Brussels.

13

I T SHOULD COME AS NO SURPRISE THAT Belgium's food combines the influences of both French and Dutch cuisine, with a good dose of German as well. Traditionally, many Belgian recipes were heavy and rustic, but today the country's restaurants are famous for serving food of French quality in German-size portions. Whatever cuisine they choose, Belgians consider good dining as one of life's greatest pleasures.

Flemish Charles de l'Ecluse played an important role in introducing the potato throughout Europe, and potatoes remain at the heart of most traditional Belgian meals. A classic if less exotic local specialty is *stoemp*, boiled potatoes mashed with a seasonal vegetable and served with ham or sausage.

Many Belgian towns also have developed their own regional specialities. Liège was the original home to the *salade Liègeoise* (sah-LAH-duh lee-a-JWAH-zuh), which combines bacon, potatoes, onions, parsley, and green beans. The Liège region is also famous for stews and soups. Ghent has contributed the famous creamy *waterzooi* (WAH-tuhr-zoohj) soup once made from fish but now just as likely from chicken. Recipes vary wildly, but, at its best, this dish is rich and creamy, and simultaneously as refreshing as a clear soup. Brussels pioneered the art of cooking with beer, as well as making the world-famous Belgian waffles. The Ardennes region is noted for game such as venison, boar,

Belgium is home to hundreds of regional cheeses, some of which are produced in old monasteries that still use traditional methods. Even the country's most classic cheeses, such as Passendale, Maredsous, and the infamously smelly Herve, are virtually unheard of outside Belgium.

and partridge, while the North Sea provides Belgium's well-known mussels and gray shrimp.

Cooking in Belgium is strongly influenced by the availability of different foods with the changing seasons. Although the globalized supply chain now makes cultivating and harvesting seasons less important than in previous eras, people still eagerly wait for the *primeurs* (pree-MEUH-rs), or early vegetables and fruits of the season, for which times restaurants organize special gastronomic events. Herrings are best in spring, May and June bring fresh asparagus and juicy strawberries, and fall marks the start of the hunting season and the arrival of wild game in the shops. Mussels are best in winter.

MARKETS VERSUS SUPERMARKETS

The pattern of shopping in Belgium has changed drastically over the last forty years or so. Small groceries, specialty shops, and markets used to be the only places that sold food and other supplies, but big supermarkets are taking more and more of the trade. Still, markets remain important as places where Belgians can find fresh food and flowers, and have an enjoyable day out. Markets are often held on Sundays, when the big malls are closed. Markets tend to be a colorful international blend, especially in cities with a high concentration of immigrants.

The Brussels Midi Market offers exotic delicacies from Italian pepper cheese and Turkish olives to African salted fish. Small stores in towns and villages offer convenience and special service. Local bakeries stock a daily range of fresh breads, rolls, pastries, and cakes. The local butcher offers all sorts of raw and cooked meats. The main street delicatessens tempt customers with displays of cold lunch meats, fish, salads, and cheeses that they will make into delicious French bread sandwiches upon request—an ideal quick and tasty lunch.

MEAT

Meat forms an important part of Belgian cuisine, and steak with french fries is probably the nation's favorite meal. Pork, rabbit meat, and chicken are

Raw ingredients for the night's cooking are often displayed on a cart or table in front of a restaurant. A seafood display is first packed with ice, then lobsters, prawns, and crabs are carefully placed within a border of fresh vegetables. An enormous fish, its mouth gaping, forms a dramatic centerpiece. Artistically decorated boards advertise the speciality of the day.

A market displays meats and cheeses.

also eaten regularly, and horsemeat is traditionally considered a delicacy (though the number of specialist horse butchers is diminishing). Various cuts of meat can be made into old-style hot pots cooked in a casserole with beer or prunes. Lamb is relatively expensive but prized, while sweetbreads, kidneys, and goose liver are considered among the most mouthwatering of luxury foods. Belgians can choose from an amazing range of sausages, many seasoned with herbs and spices. Ham and pâté from the Ardennes and salami are also popular.

Some hearty dishes are predominantly winter favorites, including *Vlaamsekarbonade* (VLAAHM-suh khar-boh-NAH-duh), a tasty beef stew cooked in a local beer. Other specialities include *faisan à la Brabanconne* (fuh-SAHN ah lah brah-bahn-SOH-nuh), pheasant braised with endive, and *konijn met pruimen* (koh-NEYHN meht PREU-muhn), rabbit cooked in beer with onions and prunes. *Ballekes* (BA-la kes), meatballs in tomato sauce, are less glamorous but remain a mainstay of traditional home cooking.

Although Americans may find it shocking, many Belgians enjoy eating horsemeat. Called paardenvlees *in Dutch and* viande chevaline *in French, the meat is made into steaks, sausages, and cold cuts. Typically a horsemeat butcher runs a shop dedicated only to horse (and donkey) and does not offer other meats. Horsemeat lovers say the flesh is delicious and nutritionally superior to beef.*

In the United States, as well as in Britain and Ireland, there is a taboo against eating horsemeat. (Slaughtering horses for food has been prohibited in the United States since 2007.) People often find the practice repulsive because they consider horses as pets, on par with dogs and cats. However, in the past, agricultural communities often looked to horsemeat for sustenance. In much of Europe—as well as in other places in the world—eating horsemeat is not unusual, but for some reason it is particularly popular in Belgium.

The difference in Western attitudes about the meat came into focus in 2013, when a huge meat scandal erupted across Europe. British inspectors found that horsemeat was being passed off as beef in many prepared food products. Even some of Burger King's hamburgers and Ikea's meatballs were found to contain horse. (This was only in Europe. The meat supply in the United States was never affected.) Millions of meatballs, sausages, burgers, and processed foods such as frozen lasagna were pulled from supermarket shelves in many countries. Even Europeans who eat horse were appalled by the fraudulent and clearly illegal labeling; and naturally, folks who don't eat horse were even more outraged.

The source of the fraud was traced to the switching of labels somewhere along the supply chain between the slaughterhouses and the food processors. Two meat trading companies, one in Cyprus and one in the Netherlands, were particularly suspect. Beef is more expensive than horse, and mixing ground beef with ground horsemeat was a way of secretly cheapening the product.

In 2015, police from seven European countries rounded up twenty-six people in a crackdown on a horsemeat trafficking ring said to be connected to the 2013 scandal. The suspects included four Belgian nationals, including the alleged ringleader.

SEAFOOD

Seafood is very popular in Belgium, and few sights are more typical than a group of diners in a seaside restaurant enjoying a steaming pot of mussels. Herbs are particularly important when cooking mussels, with onions, celery, and parsley creating that special Belgian flavor.

Belgium's North Sea gray shrimp are said to be the best in the world. A few fishers, in bright yellow oilskins, still catch these the traditional way that involves using strong Brabant horses to trawl a net through waist-high water. The most typical preparation is to boil the shrimp in salted water, shell them, and coat the flesh lightly with mayonnaise. They are then often served stuffed into a hollowed-out tomato.

Inland, river fish provide another Belgian delicacy, *paling in het groen* (PAH-ling ihn hut GROON), eel cooked in a bright green parsley sauce and served cold. Another favorite is *truite au bleu* (trweet oh bleuh), trout cooked with carrots, leeks, and potatoes, and most famously served in the idyllic Walloon village of Crupet. When the weather turns cold, street stalls around shopping areas or markets often sell freshly boiled snails in their shells as a winter warmer.

Moules-frites, or mussels with french fries, is a popular Belgian bistro dish.

SPECIAL VEGETABLES

Few cities have a vegetable named after them, but Brussels sprouts are world famous. The first record of Brussels sprouts being eaten in Belgium dates to 1587, but they were probably part of the local diet three or four centuries earlier. Sprouts grow best in cool climates and are damaged by hot weather. An excellent source of vitamins A and C, sprouts are typically a winter favorite.

Particularly prized is the Belgian asparagus, eaten in Belgium since Roman times. People favor the thick white spears and their rich flavor. The best asparagus comes from the sandy soils of the region around Mechelen.

Witloof (WHIT-loohf), or Belgian endive, is a small, rocket-shaped, leafy vegetable with white leaves with pale green tips.

Belgian endives are lined up in a basket at a produce market.

Endive is properly pronounced "on-DEEVE" in English, to differentiate it from the green, curly-leafed lettuce called "EN-dive." Belgian endive is also sometimes called chicory, because it is grown from the root of a chicory plant that has been cut and forced to grow a second time. The first growth of chicory is a curly green lettuce with a slightly bitter taste. Belgians use both the leaves as a salad and the roots as a vegetable. As a vegetable, endive is usually diced, slightly sweetened, and boiled, or wrapped whole in slices of ham and cooked in a creamy cheese sauce. Other popular vegetables include red cabbages and leeks.

WANT SOME FRIETEN WITH THAT?

Although Americans know deep-fried potatoes as french fries, the Belgians and Britons both claim to have invented them. Known in Belgium as *frieten* (FREEH-tehn, in Flemish) or *frites* (FREEH-tuh, in French), fried potatoes are a favorite Belgian street food served from mobile canteens or small huts. They are handed to customers in paper cones or on small cardboard trays. Usually, customers have them topped with a large dollop of flavored mayonnaise of which there is a bewildering variety.

Belgian *frites* have a delicious texture and flavor because they are fried twice in hot oil, first to cook the inside, then to brown and crisp the exterior. In restaurants they are served as the usual accompaniment to mussels or steak.

DAILY MEALS

Even if the family has to get to school or work, breakfast still tends to be a surprisingly relaxed mealtime. People usually sit down together and take half an hour over the meal. Breakfast is generally light: rolls, croissants, pastries, or bread with jam or cheese, and perhaps an egg washed down with coffee, or some tea, milk, or hot chocolate.

Although many restaurants offer special lunch menus, it is common for working Belgians to simply snack on a French-bread sandwich from a *traiteur* (tray-TER), or delicatessen.

Dinner is usually the main meal of the day. Although in restaurants Belgians typically display a wide range of tastes in and an appreciation for international cuisines, most home-cooked meals are relatively simple, consisting of potatoes with meatballs in tomato sauce, chicken with applesauce, or perhaps a simple spaghetti.

Traditionally, Sunday lunch is the most important meal of the week. It is a time for the family and relatives to sit together in a relaxed atmosphere. Several dishes, desserts, and drinks may be served throughout the afternoon.

DESSERTS

A nation with such great love for food is naturally going to be an expert when it comes to desserts. Some desserts are traditionally associated with towns or regions. For example, *kletskoppen* (KLEH-ts-koh-puhn), crunchy sweet cookies, originally came from Bruges, and *tarte al d'jote* (TAHRT ahl DJOH-tuh), a tart from Nivelles that is made of beet leaves and cheese. Ghent has special little cakes called *Gentse mokken* (GHENT-suh MOHK-kun), and Brussels contributes its famous Belgian waffles, served with sugar, butter, fresh cream, or fresh fruit, or both.

Chocolate pralines are heaped in a bakery window.

Favorites include sugar tart, chocolate mousse, white cheesecake, and speculoos, a typical crunchy gingerbread cookie popularly served with coffee. *Dame blanche* (DHAM BLAHNSJ) is another favorite made of vanilla ice cream with hot chocolate sauce poured across the top when served.

Juicy red strawberries, most famously grown at Wépion, have a special place in Belgian desserts and can be served with cream or used to decorate other desserts. Strawberries are now available through much of the year because special farms grow them in greenhouses, but the most productive strawberry season is in June and July.

Belgian chocolate is world famous. The extremely high standards and melt-in-the-mouth textures are maintained by using only 100 percent cocoa butter. In a café it is common to receive a small, individually wrapped square of chocolate with your coffee. For wrapped chocolate, the most common brand is Côte d'Or. However, Belgium also has a huge number of specialist chocolate shops selling handmade, bite-size pralines (prah-LEEHN). These have a vast variety of creamy, nutty, or fruity centers. The pralines are displayed like precious items in a jewelry shop and are sold by weight. As many are made with fresh cream, they cannot be kept long, although that is seldom a problem.

A BEER TO EVERYONE'S TASTE

Beer is Belgium's national beverage. There are hundreds of brands and roughly a dozen different types of beer. Standard beers (5 percent alcohol) are mostly clear lagers such as Stella Artois and unfiltered "white" beers such as the classic Hoegaarten with its hints of citrus and spice. There are also red beers, brown beers, "Scotch" beers, wheat beers, and very weak table beers. The latter have only 2 percent alcohol and were traditionally served to children with meals as a healthier alternative to sweet soft drinks. However, Belgium is most famous for its strong Abbey beers and other intensely flavored special brews that mostly have alcohol levels between 7 and 12 percent. For centuries monasteries were a great source of brews, and, even today, the most prized ales are made by monks. Just seven beers qualify for the prestigious label "Trappist." Of these, Chimay and Orval are the best known, but magnificently complex Westvleteren is probably the most sought after, being bottled only in tiny quantities.

The area southwest of Brussels, called Pajottenland (pah-JOHT-tuhn-land), is famous for its unique self-fermenting beers called *lambik* (lahm-BEEHK). Wheat and barley are left for one night in open wooden tubs while natural fermentation starts from wild yeasts. At this stage a few wild hops that grow in the region are added. The brews are then left to mature in the barrels. The result is a golden-colored beer, but the taste is like that of astringent apple juice, so *lambiks* are usually blended to make a more palatable beer called *gueuze* (GER-z) or combined with fruit. Cherries can be added for *kriek* (creek), raspberries for *framboise* (from-BWAAZ) or, less commonly, blueberries for *myrtille* (meer-TEEy).

INTERNET LINKS

belgium.beertourism.com/food/chocolate
Here, find a very complete overview of Belgian chocolate.

www.huffingtonpost.com/2014/01/21/belgian-cuisine-food_n_4617498.html
This article offers a gallery of famous Belgian dishes.

www.nytimes.com/2015/06/14/travel/in-belgiums-strawberry-fields-perfections-in-the-picking.html?ref=topics&_r=0
This article is about strawberry growing in Belgium.

CHICON AU GRATIN / GEGRATINEERDE WITLOOF (BELGIAN ENDIVE AND HAM GRATIN)

This is a popular winter dish in Belgium.

8 endives, root trimmed, but intact
4 tablespoons (60 grams) butter
8 slices lean deli-style ham
2 tablespoons all-purpose flour
2 cups (475 milliliters) whole milk, hot but not boiling
freshly cracked black pepper, for seasoning
⅛ teaspoon freshly grated nutmeg
2 cups (8 ounces) (230 g) grated gruyere cheese

Butter a 9 by 13-inch (33 by 23 cm) baking dish. Preheat oven to 375°F (190°C).

Steam or simmer endives in a covered pot until soft but not mushy, about 10 or 15 minutes. Drain with leaves pointing down, gently squeezing endives with clean kitchen towel to dry and expel as much water as possible. (Watery endives will ruin the dish.)

In a large frying pan over medium-high heat, melt 2 tablespoons of the butter. Add the endives and cook, turning occasionally, until lightly brown on all sides. Remove from heat and roll one slice of ham around each endive. Set into prepared dish.

In a small saucepan over medium heat, melt 2 tablespoons of butter. Whisk in the flour and cook 1 minute, being careful not to brown the flour. Slowly whisk in the milk until smooth. Reduce heat to medium-low and simmer until thickened, about 8 minutes. Season with pepper and nutmeg.

Pour the sauce over the endives and sprinkle with the cheese. Bake until the cheese is melted and the sauce is bubbling, about 30 minutes. Broil until the cheese lightly browns, about 2 minutes. Serve hot with mashed potatoes, if desired.

SPECULOOS / SPECULAAS (BELGIAN SPICE COOKIES)

These cookies are traditionally served on St. Nicholas's Day, December 6.

1 ¾ cup (210 g) all purpose flour
¼ teaspoon *each* baking soda and salt
2 ½ teaspoon ground cinnamon
¾ teaspoon *each* ground nutmeg and cloves
½ teaspoon ground ginger
¼ teaspoon *each* ground white pepper and black pepper
¼ teaspoon ground cardamom
½ cup (1 stick or 120 g) unsalted butter, room temperature
1 cup (180 g) light brown sugar
1 large egg
1 ½ teaspoon vanilla

NOTE: These are traditionally made with cookie molds or a springerle rolling pin, which is embossed with designs. They can also be made with cookie cutters or cut into rectangles.

In a medium-sized bowl, whisk together the flour, baking soda, salt, and spices. Set aside. In a large bowl, beat the butter, sugar, and vanilla until light. Add the egg and vanilla and beat until fluffy. Gradually add the dry ingredients mixture and beat just until well combined. (If using a stand mixer, use the paddle attachment.)
Split the dough in half. Wrap each piece in plastic and chill at least one hour.
Line a baking sheet with parchment paper. If using the springerle rolling pin, use a plain rolling pin to roll the dough out until ½-inch thick. Liberally dust the springerle pin with flour then roll over the dough, pressing firmly to make a ¼-inch-thick cookie dough, with imprint. Cut the dough along the springerle grid lines with a sharp knife or pizza cutter and place on baking sheet. If you don't have a springerle pin, roll dough to ¼-inch thick and cut with cookie cutters. Chill the baking sheet with uncooked cookies for 30 minutes.

Meanwhile, preheat the oven to 375°F (190°C). Bake the cookies in the oven 9 to 11 minutes or until golden brown on the edges. Let the cookies cool on the baking sheet for 10 minutes, then move to wire rack to cool. The cookies harden as they cool.

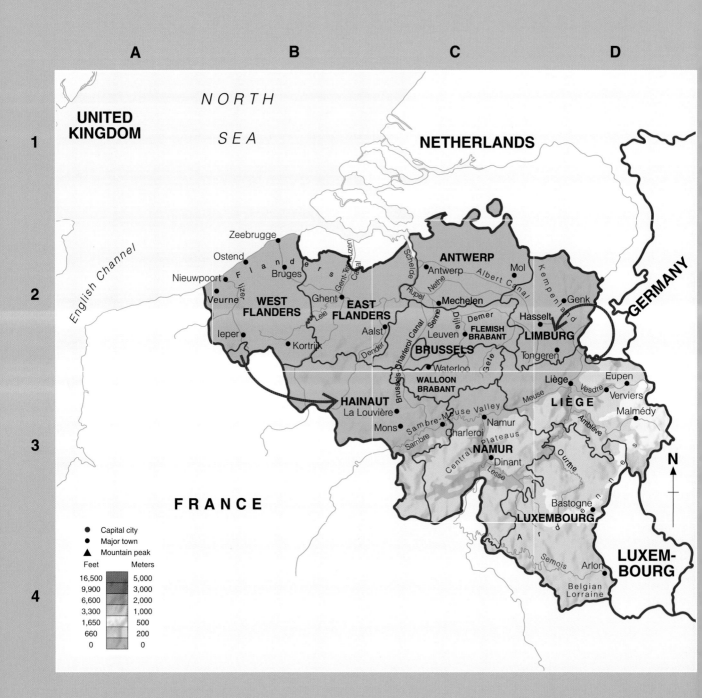

A   **B**   **C**   **D**

1

NORTH

UNITED KINGDOM

SEA

NETHERLANDS

English Channel

Zeebrugge

Ostend

Nieuwpoort

F l a n d e r s

Bruges

Gent-Terneuzen Canal

Schelde

ANTWERP

Antwerp

Nethe

Mol

Albert Canal

Kempenland

GERMANY

2

Veurne

Ijzer

WEST FLANDERS

Ghent

Leie

EAST FLANDERS

Rupel

Mechelen

Senne

Dijle

Demer

Genk

Hasselt

Ieper

Aalst

Leuven

FLEMISH BRABANT

LIMBURG

Kortrijk

Dender

BRUSSELS

Tongeren

Waterloo

Gete

Liège

Vesdre

Eupen

Verviers

WALLOON BRABANT

Meuse

LIÈGE

Malmédy

HAINAUT

La Louvière

Brussels-Charleroi Canal

Mons

Sambre-Meuse Valley

Namur

Amblève

Sambre

Charleroi

Central Plateaus

Ourthe

3

NAMUR

Dinant

Lesse

Bastogne

LUXEMBOURG

N

FRANCE

- Capital city
- Major town
- ▲ Mountain peak

Feet	Meters
16,500	5,000
9,900	3,000
6,600	2,000
3,300	1,000
1,650	500
660	200
0	0

Semois

Arlon

Belgian Lorraine

LUXEMBOURG

4

MAP OF BELGIUM

ECONOMIC BELGIUM

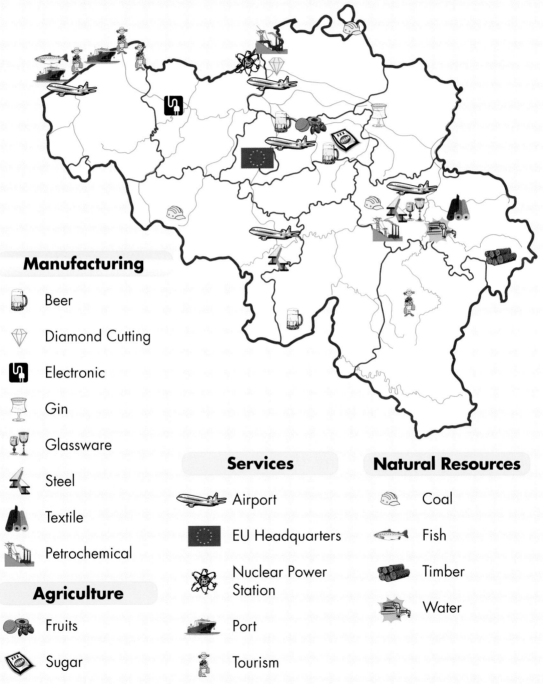

Manufacturing

🍺 Beer

💎 Diamond Cutting

🔌 Electronic

🍷 Gin

🍷 Glassware

⚒️ Steel

🛢️ Textile

🏭 Petrochemical

Agriculture

🍒 Fruits

🍬 Sugar

Services

✈️ Airport

🇪🇺 EU Headquarters

⚛️ Nuclear Power Station

🚢 Port

🧳 Tourism

Natural Resources

⛑️ Coal

🐟 Fish

🪵 Timber

💧 Water

ABOUT THE ECONOMY

GROSS DOMESTIC PRODUCT (GDP)
$481 billion (2014)

GDP GROWTH
1 percent (2014)

GDP BY SECTOR
Agriculture 0.8 percent, industry 21.1 percent, services 78.1 percent (2014)

INFLATION RATE
0.5 percent (2014)

CURRENCY
Euro = 100 Euro cents
Notes: 5, 10, 20, 50, 100, 500 Euros
Coins: 1, 2 Euros; 1, 2, 5, 10, 20, 50 Euro cents
USD1 = 0.92 Euros (November 2015)

AGRICULTURAL PRODUCTS
Sugar beets, fresh vegetables, fruits, grain, tobacco; beef, veal, pork, milk

MAJOR EXPORTS
Chemicals, machinery and equipment, finished diamonds, metals and metal products, foodstuffs

MAJOR IMPORTS
Raw materials, machinery and equipment, chemicals, raw diamonds, pharmaceuticals, foodstuffs, transportation equipment, oil products

MAIN TRADE PARTNERS
Germany, France, Netherlands, United Kingdom, United States, Italy (2014)

LABOR FORCE
5.225 million (2014)

LABOR FORCE BY OCCUPATION
Agriculture 1.3 percent, industry 18.6 percent, services 80.1 percent (2013)

UNEMPLOYMENT RATE
8.5 percent (2014)

INTERNET USERS
9.5 million (2014)

CULTURAL BELGIUM

Bruges
The "Venice of the North," it is one of the most charming old cities in Europe.

Ghent
It has a genuine, lived-in feel despite a superbly picturesque old center, a moated castle, and some of the nation's most atmospheric cafés.

Scherpenheuvel
Dominated by its multisided, star-spangled domes church, this is Belgium's greatest pilgrimage site.

Waterloo
A bronze lion tops a conical grassy mound, marking the site of Europe's most famous battlefield.

Zoutleeuw
This forgotten little village has a dramatic town hall and the most perfectly preserved church interior in Belgium.

Tongeren
Belgium's oldest town has an attractive town square. Roman ruins and a prominent weekly antiques market can be found here.

Brussels
A vibrant city where art nouveau and surrealism live alongside the modern-day EU capital, it is also famous for its wonderful chocolate shops.

Carnivals
Of all Belgium's great carnivals, Binche hosts the most typical with its trademark Giles throwing oranges, donning spooky masks, and wearing unbeatably photogenic costumes.

Castles
Belgium has dozens of famous castles. Stately Beloeil, intriguing moated Horst, and historic, medieval Bouillon are all fascinating and each entirely different in style.

Rochefort and Han-Sur-Lesse
This area is famed for extensive cave systems. At Han-Sur-Lesse the underground visit is by tram.

ABOUT THE CULTURE

OFFICIAL NAME
Kingdom of Belgium (English), Belgique (French), België (Flemish), Belgien (German)

NATIONAL FLAG
Three equal vertical stripes of black (left), yellow or gold, and red.

TOTAL AREA
11,786 square miles (30,528 sq km)

CAPITAL
Brussels

POPULATION
11,323,973 (July 2015)

POPULATION GROWTH RATE
0.76 percent (2015)

ETHNO-LINGUISTIC GROUPS
Flemish 58 percent, Walloon 31 percent, mixed or other 11 percent

MAIN LANGUAGES
Dutch 60 percent, French 40 percent, German less than 1 percent (all are official).

MAJOR RELIGIONS
Roman Catholic 75 percent, 6 percent Islam, Protestant 1.7 percent, Jewish, 0.27 percent; other or none 17 percent

BIRTH RATE
11.41 births per 1,000 population (2015)

DEATH RATE
9.63 deaths per 1,000 population (2015)

AGE DISTRIBUTION
0 to 14 years: 17 percent
15 to 64 years: 65 percent
65 years and over: 18 percent

LITERACY RATE
99 percent

NATIONAL HOLIDAYS
New Year's Day (January 1), Labor Day (May 1), Flemish Community Day (July 11, not in Wallonia), Easter Monday (dates vary), National Day (July 21), the Assumption (August 15), Francophone Community Day (September 27, not in Flanders), All Saints' Day (November 1), Armistice Day (November 11), German Community Day (November 15), Christmas Day (December 25)

LEADERS IN POLITICS
King Philippe, constitutional monarch (since 2013)
Charles Michel, prime minister (since 2014)

TIMELINE

IN BELGIUM	IN THE WORLD

1500 BCE
Celts and Franks start to settle the region.

753 BCE
Rome is founded.

116–117 BCE
The Roman Empire reaches its greatest extent.

52 BCE
Centurians defeat the Belgae tribe. The region becomes part of the Roman Empire.

CE 600
Height of Mayan civilization.

768–814 CE
Reign of Charlemagne

1000
The Chinese perfect gunpowder and begin to use it in warfare.

1302
Flemish citizens defeat French knights at the Battle of the Golden Spurs.

1384–1451
The dukes of Burgundy take control.

1506
The region comes under Spanish or Hapsburg rule.

1530
Beginning of transatlantic slave trade.

1558–1603
Reign of Elizabeth I of England.

1585
Future Belgium returns to Spanish rule.

1620
Pilgrims sail the *Mayflower* to America.

1648
Antwerp's port is closed following the Eighty Years War.

1695
French forces bombard Brussels, destroying the Grand Place and stealing the Manneken Pis.

1714–1794
Austrian rule

1776
US Declaration of Independence is signed.

1790–1792
The Brabanconne Revolution declares the United States of Belgium.

1789–1799
The French Revolution.

1795
Belgium is annexed by revolutionary France.

1814–1830
Belgium comes under Dutch rule.

IN BELIUM	IN THE WORLD
1815 The Battle of Waterloo is waged.	
1830 Belgium gains independence.	**1861** The US Civil War begins.
1878–1908 King Leopold II develops the Congo as his personal territory.	**1869** The Suez Canal is opened.
1914–1918 World War I devastates western Flanders.	**1914** World War I begins.
1939–1945 World War II: Belgium is occupied by Nazi Germany.	**1939–1945** World War II.
	1949 The North Atlantic Treaty Organization (NATO) is formed.
1962 Linguistic frontier is formalized between Flemish- and French-speaking communities. Belgian Congo gains independence.	**1966–1969** The Chinese Cultural Revolution.
1993 The death of King Baudouin creates brief unity between linguistic regions.	**1991** Breakup of the Soviet Union.
1995 Belgium is divided into a three-part federation.	**1997** Hong Kong is returned to China.
1999 Prince Philippe marries Princess Mathilde.	
2002 Belgium sends troops to Afghanistan as part of the International Security Assistance Force.	**2001** Terrorists crash planes in New York, Washington, DC, and Pennsylvania.
2003 The Binche Carnival is declared a UNESCO masterpiece of intangible cultural heritage.	**2003** War in Iraq
2013 King Albert II abdicates throne in favor of Crown Prince Philippe.	**2008** United States elects first African American president, Barack Obama.
2015 Four tourists thwart terror attack on train from Brussels to Paris.	**2015** Turmoil in the Middle East spurs mass migration of refugees to Europe.

GLOSSARY

Begijnhoven (buh-GEYEN-hoven)
Walled community of cloistered homes where women could enjoy company and security in a religious atmosphere.

duivenmelker (DEUY-vuhn-mehl-khur)
A person who breeds pigeons to race.

federalism
A system of government in which the states or provinces share power with a national government.

frieten (Flemish, FREEH-tehn)
frites (French, FREEH-tuh)
Belgian-style french fries.

Gilles (JEEH-luh)
Participants in the Binche carnival who wear brightly colored medieval costumes. They go around town throwing oranges at the public.

La Belgitude (LAH behl-ji-TUU-duh)
Belgian art movement at the beginning of the twentieth century that developed a national feeling.

lock
A portion of a canal with gates at either end, the closing and opening of which adjusts the water level in that part of the canal.

Ommegang (OHM-muh-gang)
A historical parade held in Brussels, a reenactment of a parade held for Charles V in 1549.

polder (POHL-duhr)
An area in Flanders Lowlands region consisting of thin, sandy soil, with clay underneath.

primeurs (pree-MEUH-rs)
Vegetables and fruits eaten at the very beginning of their season.

speculoos (SPEH-kuh-loohs)
Crunchy gingerbread cookies.

taalvrijheid (TAAHL-vreye-heyet)
The right to use Flemish as an official language, claimed by the Flemish.

tarte al d'jote (TARHT ahl DJOH-tuh)
Typical Walloon flan made of beet leaves and cheese.

Walloon (wah-LOHN)
A group of French dialects spoken in Wallonia, with origins in the old Celtic and Germanic languages.

waterzooi (WAH-tuhr-zoohj)
Typical Flemish dish, made of fish or chicken in a soup with potatoes, carrots, leeks, and cream.

witloof (WHIT-loohf)
Belgian endive, a form of chicory bud, that is a popular white vegetable used in salad or cooked.

FOR FURTHER INFORMATION

BOOKS

Deem, James M. *The Prisoners of Breendonk: Personal Histories from a World War II Concentration Camp*. New York: Houghton Mifflin, 2015.

DK Publishing. *Eyewitness Travel Guide: Belgium & Luxembourg*. New York: DK Publishing, 2015.

Elliott, Mark. *Culture Shock! Belgium*. London: Kuperard, 2002.

Hochschild, Adam. *King Leopold's Ghost: A Story of Greed, Terror, and Heroism in Colonial Africa*. New York: Houghton Mifflin, 1999.

Van Waerebeek-Gonzalez, Ruth. *Everybody Eats Well in Belgium Cookbook*. New York: Workman Publishing, 1996.

WEBSITES

BBC News. Belgium country profile. www.bbc.com/news/world-europe-17205436

Belgium.be. www.belgium.be/en

CIA World Factbook. Belgium. www.cia.gov/library/publications/the-world-factbook/geos/be.html

European Union. Belgium. europa.eu/about-eu/countries/member-countries/belgium/index_en.htm

Flanders Online www.flanders.be/en

Lonely Planet. Belgium. www.lonelyplanet.com/belgium

New York Times, The. Times Topics. Belgium. topics.nytimes.com/top/news/international/countriesandterritories/belgium/index.html

Wallonia Online www.wallonia.be/en

BIBLIOGRAPHY

BBC News. Belgium country profile. http://www.bbc.com/news/world-europe-17205436.

BBC iWonder. "The Battle of Waterloo: The day that decided Europe's fate." http://www.bbc.co.uk/timelines/zwtf34j.

Carvajal, Doreen. "Catholics in Belgium Start Parishes of Their Own." *New York Times*, November 16, 2010. http://www.nytimes.com/2010/11/17/world/europe/17iht-belgium.html.

CIA World Factbook. Belgium. http://www.cia.gov/library/publications/the-world-factbook/geos/be.html.

City of Brussels. http://www.brussels.be/artdet.cfm.

Cody, Edward. "Horsemeat scandal dents Europe's culinary self-image." *Washington Post*, February 26, 2013. https://www.washingtonpost.com/world/europe/horsemeat-scandal-dents-europes-culinary-self-image/2013/02/26/882393fe-801c-11e2-b99e-6baf4ebe42df_story.html.

European Union. http://europa.eu.

Hackett, Conrad. "5 facts about the Muslim population in Europe." *Pew Research Center*, November 17, 2015. http://www.pewresearch.org/fact-tank/2015/11/17/5-facts-about-the-muslim-population-in-europe.

Internet World Stats. http://www.internetworldstats.com/europa.htm.

Liphshiz, Cnaan. "Divided Belgium finally admits Holocaust complicity." *The Times of Israel*, January 22, 2013. http://www.timesofisrael.com/divided-belgium-finally-admits-holocaust-complicity.

Spiegel, Alison. "How You Pronounce 'Endive' Actually Matters, And Here's Why." *Huffington Post*, March 13, 2015. http://www.huffingtonpost.com/2015/03/13/how-do-you-pronounce-endive_n_6859086.html.

Stack, Liam. "How Belgium Became Home to Recent Terror Plots." *The New York Times*, November 15, 2015. http://www.nytimes.com/interactive/2015/11/15/world/europe/belgium-terrorism-suspects.html.

Watson, Ivan, and Antonia Mortensen. "Toxic mix that makes Belgium fertile ground for terrorism." *CNN*, January 22, 2015. http://www.cnn.com/2015/01/22/europe/belgium-terror-recruiting.

Zaougui, Chams Eddine. "Molenbeek, Belgium's 'Jihad Central.'" *New York Times*, November 19, 2015. http://www.nytimes.com/2015/11/19/opinion/molenbeek-belgiums-jihad-central.html?_r=0.

INDEX

INDEX